MY LIFE AS A SPY

Born in Glasgow in 1937, LESLIE WOODHEAD is one of Britain's most distinguished documentary film-makers. His pioneering films, often on major Eastern European themes, have won many awards, including a BAFTA and the Royal Television Society award. He was also awarded an OBE for 'services to television'. He lives in Cheshire.

LESLIE WOODHEAD

MY LIFE AS A SPY

PAN BOOKS

First published 2005 by Macmillan

First published in paperback 2006 by Pan Books
an imprint of Pan Macmillan Ltd
Pan Macmillan, 20 New Wharf Road, London N1 9RR
Basingstoke and Oxford
Associated companies throughout the world
www.panmacmillan.com

ISBN-13: 978-0-330-42646-6
ISBN-10: 0-330-42646-X

9 8 7 6 5 4 3 2 1

A CIP catalogue record for this book is available from
the British Library.

Typeset by SetSystems Ltd, Saffron Walden, Essex
Printed and bound in Great Britain by
Mackays of Chatham plc, Chatham, Kent

All Pan Macmillan titles are available from
www.panmacmillan.com
or from Bookpost by telephoning +44 (0)1624 677237

FOR JAMES AND ALISON

Acknowledgements

I would like to thank the ranks of fellow linguists who were generous with their advice and their memories: Geoffrey Elliott and Harold Shukman, Graham Boiling and the East Neuk Luncheon Club, Gerry Smith, Ted Braun, Kenith Trodd, Michael Frayn and Alan Bennett. My thanks also to Professor Richard Aldrich.

I FOUND a snapshot the other day: a grave, narrow-faced boy with big ears and a tie which seemed to have been used as a tow rope. This had once been me, a solitary child during the monochrome years after World War II, living in the heart of a northern city, soot-blackened to a Lowry silhouette. It must have been about this time that I discovered the curious satisfactions of espionage.

I lived above my parents' music shop in a flat which rambled up through three floors, echoing to the wheezing complaints of sick accordions being restored to health at the patient hands of my father. I avoided the upper floors, nervous of the spooky, unvisited spaces. A broken window had allowed one room to become carpeted with dead pigeons.

In the sunless valley between our kitchen, where we had to keep the light on all day, and the looming wall of a neighbouring covered market, blank and impenetrable as a prison, there was a narrow balcony. This little thoroughfare, with flats down one side facing the wall of the market, was like a leftover Victorian community where families snuggled up with commerce.

The market was my patch. I haunted the arcades and alleyways, sheltered by the soaring roof with its flamboyant cast-iron trelliswork and buttresses, a child dwarfed by a cathedral of trade built for a more confident age eighty years earlier. I knew the ripe smells of black pudding and vegetables and boiled sweets – still rationed in those years after the war. I filled the void with bags of unrationed Chlorodine cough drops, available from Mr Beevers at my favourite stall under a hoarding which declared his was 'The Little Firm with the Big Push'. A market butcher with a face as raw as his sides of beef recruited me for his village cricket team. At home in this world of grown-ups, I timed my walks from my mother's record shop to the bus stop by the ornate market clock under the central dome.

WE LIVED AT 22 Market Balcony, and the strip of tarmac outside our door, which always seemed to be wet with recent rain, was my playground. I spent hours and days bouncing a tennis ball off the wall and belting it to imaginary boundaries in my quest to follow my cricketing hero, Len Hutton. My other obsession was the spyhole.

One day I spotted a gap in the wall. A small fragment had fallen away and I put my eye to the peephole.

It is hard now, more than fifty years later, to recover the sources of my excitement. The object of my snooping was, after all, no more than the shabby collection of stalls selling utility shirts and blouses, tough meat and dusty vegetables. But tracking the comings and goings of stallholders and shoppers, I felt special. It wasn't that

I witnessed black market deals or furtive lovers. Nothing even vaguely memorable ever happened. But I could see them, while they were totally unaware I was watching.

It seems to me that those boyish snoopings had some of the ingredients which have made Britons peculiarly well suited to the dubious arts of spying: an evasive detachment, a quiet duplicity, perhaps an unstated sense of superiority. And always, those layers of irony and self-deprecation which are held to be the essential ingredients of every British stereotype – as essential to the spying trade as invisible ink or a hidden camera.

However that may be, my peephole led on to a temporary passion for spy toys like the fabulous Seebackroscope, a cheap plastic monocle which gave me a blurred and pointless glimpse of the non-events going on behind my back. My constant companion, a book called *101 Things a Boy Can Make*, offered plans for a 'secret intercom radio'; but that required access to a used cigar box, and I had never seen such an exotic object. Soon I discovered new enthusiasms – stargazing and devising elaborate interplanetary cricket competitions. My boyhood spying obsession faded.

In the spring of 1956, aged eighteen, like 2 million other young men of my generation, I received a buff envelope. The summons to serve Her Majesty with two years of military service signalled the end of boyhood. It was also the beginning of what I've come to call 'my life as a spy'.

But this story begins long before then – with a boy in wartime.

PART ONE

SNOOPING

1

IT HAD BEEN an odd sort of childhood. My birth in pre-war Glasgow marked the end of a previously care-free passage in my parents' lives. As a child, exploring cluttered drawers in our suburban council house, I came upon evidence of those vanished years. Maybe it was something to do with the isolation of being an only child, this need to pursue a kind of espionage on my own parents, looking for fragments of intelligence which no one else could provide.

The yellowed snaps I found in the drawer gave me glimpses of a man and a woman I could hardly recognize. The parents I knew were like other parents – solid, quiet, unremarkable. This couple were the people I had dimly heard about, bohemians from the 1920s and 30s when my father was on the road as a dance band saxophonist, a member of a raffish outfit called Sid Seymour and his Mad Hatters.

Through the eyes of a wartime child, those photographs seemed impossibly glamorous. My father, lean and handsome in a dinner jacket, gazes at the camera with a confident smile, my mother beside him, pretty in a beret, looks happy and free of troubles. Another snap captures my father with the band on a stairway, like a 1920s rehearsal of the Beatles' first album cover. In yet another, he is in a line-up with the rest of the Mad Hatters, legs raised like showgirls, hands on one another's shoulders. The sun seems always to be shining.

My arrival put a stop to all that. My father quit the road and opened a music shop in the middle of Glasgow with a banjo-playing colleague. My mother swapped a leisured existence in a carefree sequence of boarding-houses for the responsibilities of raising me. She always spoke of that lost life with a dreamy smile. It was only thirty years later that I discovered a clue about how hard she found her new life as a mother.

Searching for a screwdriver in a drawer at my parents' house, I found a letter dated December 1937. I would have been four months old when the doctor wrote to my parents. In his impeccable copperplate handwriting, he suggested that, since baby Leslie was perfectly well, it was surely time now for my mother to have me home from the nursing-home where I had been born. The doctor hoped my mother was now feeling able to cope. Reading that letter, I had a stab of memory. I recalled rushing home from toddlers' school excited about show-ing my mother the medal I had won for assembling the alphabet while the other kids played in a sandpit. Out-side our house, I saw my mother being stretchered into an ambulance watched by wide-eyed children from next door. There were bewildering murmurs about her 'con-dition', and an aunt was summoned from Yorkshire. It was weeks before my mother came home. No one told me what had been wrong with her.

The sense of things not said and secrets withheld, of something going on that was not to be talked about, was always there as I was growing up. I suppose I thought the answers might be in some overstuffed drawer, or in an adult conversation I couldn't quite hear. The contraceptives I once came upon looked like sad deflated balloons, but something told me even then it was best not to ask what they were for.

My earliest memories are of watching and listening. It seemed to connect somehow with the spooky propaganda posters that were everywhere in those years when the wooden wireless spilled out only stories of war. I can see those posters now, a surreal montage of ears and mouths and the message: 'Loose talk costs lives.'

My father had left the Glasgow music shop to work as an armaments inspector during the war, coming home with exquisite technical drawings of bombs and shells. The drawings joined the other secrets stored in the house, along with the micrometers in their velvet-lined boxes.

For me, World War II is a series of disconnected snapshots. Workmen arrive to cut down our iron railings and haul them away to fuel the war effort; playing on the street, I am a British soldier pursuing a boy from next door who says he's a Russian; in the back garden, I make a magical discovery – a silver fragment, heavy and mysterious, shrapnel from an overnight bomb; in our air-raid shelter, my mother tries to make a game of pulling on my Mickey Mouse gas mask; I find a chromium revolver in a drawer, and my father hurries away in a fluster to throw it in a nearby canal; on our way to the air-raid shelter I look up to see searchlights stabbing a swastika on the wing of a plane roaring horribly close overhead; one evening, kids are dancing round a lamppost on our street chanting, 'The war's over, the war's over.'

For all the unanswered questions, I was happy. Foraging for whatever sparse materials he could track down, my father made thrilling models for me, planes and ships and cars. A Westland Lysander, the aircraft which had landed secret agents in French fields, touched down in my bedroom. Best of all, he came home with a Bingoscope, an intriguing black box with a silver handle that could perform miracles. Those evenings when we dragged out the Bingoscope and laced a little wheel of film into its guts never lost their excitement for me. Mickey Mouse and Charlie Chaplin and Popeye flickered into life on a bedsheet as my father turned the handle. My favourite was a four-minute slapstick fragment called *The Boys Become Waiters*, joyously full of shattered dinner plates and spilled food. I never tired of asking for repeats. I unreeled the spools and studied the tiny frames where Charlie and Mickey and Popeye were trapped. The alchemy which could transform these frozen bits of time into moving pictures fascinated me.

Now the war was over, my parents wanted to return to home ground and start again. Both of them were from Yorkshire, and in Scotland I lived a strange double life. In the playground of my primary school in Glasgow, we seven-year-olds regularly organized tribal contests between 'Kilts' and 'Trousers'. I turned out for both sides. It was a split identity which did not bother me or anyone else. Tearing around my little suburban universe with scruffy Glaswegian chums my accent was as feisty as the sporran I sometimes wore with my kilt. Indoors, I switched over to match my parents' Yorkshire accents. Then suddenly, in the autumn of 1946, the choice was made for me. We were heading south.

I can still recall that journey, wobbling down the Great North Road perched on a pile of bedding in the back seat of a dodgy 1934 Hillman my father had somehow managed to pick up despite the post-war austerities. A tyre exploded with a terrifying bang somewhere in the Borders, and we arrived at Grandmother Jagger's terrace house near Leeds long after dark. I felt stranded in this strange place. I was handed a key on a string and directed to the Victorian lavatory in a yard round the back. A spider scuttled down the flaking whitewashed wall. I stumbled and cut my knee scampering back to the house.

For weeks, it seemed, while my parents went off to set up our new life, I lived in my granny's house. I spent hours lost in the pages of a huge book she kept, a bound collection of a late Victorian magazine full of lurid stories about murderers and train disasters, illustrated with pictures of heroes and freaks. I began to feel stuck in that older time which seemed to live on in the house. Granny got down on her knees every morning to spruce up her doorstep with a pumice stone in a daily campaign to outshine the neighbours. Then she dug out a tin of black lead to anoint the cooking range, making it gleam like the back of a beetle. Milk was delivered by a horse and cart, ladled from a churn by a chubby man in a bowler hat. Neighbours rushed out of their doors to shovel up the horse shit for their allotments. I got to know the smells of my granny's parlour: old perfume and boiled vegetables. The raw dankness of the lavatory in the yard always made me shiver.

Halifax, where my father had found an empty shop, was a forbidding place in that winter after the war. My first sight of my new home was bound up with an alarm that the steepling hill down into the town would burn out the brakes of the old Hillman. I grabbed the back of my mother's seat, somehow imagining I could save us from a plunge into the murky pit below, spiked with black chimneys. Rattling at last into the town centre, I felt the weight of the big bald hillside we had just survived, looming over everything like the brow of a watching ogre. Every building in the old wool town seemed to have been dutifully blackened like Granny's stove.

Granny's lurid magazine had told me that for hundreds of years Halifax maintained a notorious gibbet, where scores of petty thieves had been executed. Long before the French Revolution, the magazine salivated, the Halifax gibbet, known as 'the Scottish Maiden', had pioneered the ghoulish technology for chopping off heads. Now I saw a sign for 'Gibbet Street'. Years later, I came across a medieval prayer: 'From Hell, Hull and Halifax, Good Lord deliver us.' On that gloomy day in

1946, I felt much the same way about my new home town.

The shop had been abandoned for years, and my first sight of it was of a dispiriting room piled with broken furniture, entombed in dust. For some reason, scores of discarded spectacles littered the floor. I wondered how my parents could ever bring this place back to life.

The flat over the shop which was to be my new home seemed cold and sinister. As though they shared my unease about the warren of rooms on the upper floors, my parents crammed our lives into the territory just above the shop. Huddling like refugees in an abandoned building, we occupied just three rooms. My bed was set up in my parents' bedroom, where buses roared past the window day and night, and the mound of bedclothes which was my sleeping mother and father was my first sight every morning. This curious arrangement persisted for years, until the unspoken embarrassment of early teenage stirred me to move out. I ventured up one floor to establish my bedroom alongside the family bath. The sense of distorted domestic geography seeped into my life in this strange place, so that it seemed odd, somehow off centre, not like other families.

In the first months of 1947, dirty snowdrifts stood like concrete barriers on the streets for weeks. I hated my new school, where I was the subject of a variety of unsubtle extortion rackets – 'Give me your apple, or I'll bash you!' I resented having to swap my friends from Whitburn Street in Glasgow for those solitary games on Market Balcony. I did not want to be there.

But the new music shop – 'Fred Woodhead, The Music Man' painted on the window – prospered as Britain began to crawl out of the post-war cave of rationing and shortages. I remember that Harry James and his band blaring through 'Flight of the Bumble Bee' was the big seller for weeks in those innocent pre-Elvis days.

Soon Harry James was left behind. New sounds drifted up the stairs from the shop to the living-room where I was failing to practise the piano in a rare gesture of rebellion. Now it was Johnny Ray and Frankie Laine and their paler British shadows Dickie Valentine and Lita Rosa. My father sold sheet music and instruments from a shop counter he had made himself and covered in brown lino. He stored the huge stock of music in unmarked files, memorizing every item. Piano teachers who haunted the shop were regularly amazed that he could locate some obscure piece – 'Bless This House' in the key of three flats – in moments. I sensed that he took pride in the fact that only he could find his way through the maze he had created. And of course it made his constant presence in the shop inescapable.

MY MOTHER ran the record shop, storing the big 78 rpm discs in orange boxes. Her domain was a tiny hutch lined with white tiles which must once have been a butcher's stall. Crammed into a corner with a record player, she dealt with her fractious clientele. 'They don't know the title, they don't know the artist, but they expect me to know what they want,' she lamented. But as 'pop music' began to take off in the early 50s, the little shop was increasingly besieged by the newly liberated teenagers with a few shillings to spend. My mother needed help. She was joined behind the counter by Brenda, a buxom girl who became the unknowing focus of my pre-pubescent yearnings as I hung around the shop.

Every lunchtime, my hard-pressed mother dashed upstairs and made something for me, since I refused to stay for meals at school. I was aware it was daily agony for her, pulled between the shop and me. I suppose turning up needlessly every lunchtime was my fumbled expression of resentment for being brought to this unwanted place. My reward was beans and chips every day for five years.

In the autumn of 1948, plucked out via the chancy selection of the eleven plus examination, I was translated to a boys' grammar school with a Latin motto over the gate. There was a rumour that the chilly outhouse which served as the school lavatory was of Tudor vintage. Whatever the truth of that, the academic syllabus maintained a diet unchanged since the time of Tom Brown's school days: Latin, Greek, supervised by masters in gowns, and rugger – all sustained by the prospect of caning. The headmaster was a former army officer with a moustache modelled on Field Marshal Montgomery's and a bark to match. I got my mother to devise weekly notes excusing me from the horrors of rugger.

But I slogged dutifully over Ovid and Homer, and the dusty French tragedies of Racine and Corneille. Then I found a mentor. Eric Taylor was a quiet, unworldly man who informed his Shakespeare class, drowsing over *Midsummer Night's Dream*, that he liked 'a nice dry Bottom' and seemed oblivious to the stifled giggles. But gradually Mr Taylor got my attention. Intrigued by the boldness of John Donne and thrilled by the verbal gymnastics of Gerard Manley Hopkins, those English lessons became something special for me. Meanwhile, the thrice daily trek between school and Market Balcony defined my days. It seemed that nothing could ever change.

Though it certainly didn't seem that way at the time, for me the possibility that things might be different began with a teacher bustling into my classroom. With the self-importance of a bearer of grave news, he announced, 'I'm very sorry to tell you, boys, that King George has passed away.' I knew it was important, and that I ought to feel sad. But this was half a century away from Elton John lamenting Princess Diana, and piled flowers at Buckingham Palace. The Royal Family were distant demigods on a balcony, deference was the national mode, tabloid-fuelled voyeurism was unthinkable. Radio abandoned all programmes for days, sombre music flooded the airwaves. Still, something I had always thought was for ever had shifted.

Then, one afternoon in May 1953, a man brought a television set into our house. He fixed it up in the gloomy kitchen, and switched on for the first time. The nine-inch screen blossomed into life. It was Children's Hour on BBC Television – a programme called *Whirligig*, featuring a crude puppet with a turnip's head, and his chum, a chap in a waistcoat, Humphrey Lestocq, known as 'HL'. Mr Turnip's strings got tangled, HL fluffed his lines, the picture wobbled. I was entranced.

For a fifteen-year-old boy living in industrial Yorkshire, the idea that I might enter that exotic world glowing on the television screen was unimaginable. That was for other people, people like the men with bow ties and posh voices who appeared on *What's My Line?*, or the women announcers who sounded like the Queen. The TV news was just another posh voice, reading over a photo of Nelson's column. But it was thrilling to have this miracle in our kitchen. When *Panorama* started, with Richard Dimbleby in his three-piece suit telling us about the war in Korea, they called it 'A Window on the World'. That's just how it felt on Market Balcony.

Like millions of other Britons, my parents had admitted television into their lives just in time to watch the coronation of the new Queen. Friends and family came from miles away to watch the spectacle on our TV, munching sandwiches and vowing to get a set of their own. An aunt with pretensions, determined to have a bigger screen than the neighbours, bought one of the new magnifying gadgets you could strap on the front of the television. I thought it was like peering through a fish tank. Then she invested in a hilarious invention which promised to make your black and white picture burst into colour. It was just a bit of plastic she stuck on the screen, blue at the top, brown in the middle and green at the bottom. On the rare occasions when the television was showing a picture of a desert island, it might have lent a smudgy novelty value. For the rest of the time, my aunt got used to announcers with blue foreheads and green chins.

It was still the early 50s, a world so removed from the pace and profusion we take for granted now that it is sometimes hard to make the connections. The single black and white channel was presented by announcers in dinner jackets and ballgowns, dreamy 'Interludes' dawdled through the long gaps between programmes: a kitten playing with a ball of wool, a man throwing wood on a bonfire. Closedown was around 10 p.m., when the nation was dispatched to unheated bedrooms with the strains of the national anthem. Marriage was for ever, divorce unimaginable, homosexuals were unmentionable criminals. Train drivers were heroes of steam, smog was as inevitable as snow in winter. My father arranged to have all his teeth pulled in his thirties 'because it would mean less fuss later'. I sat in the car waiting for him, and saw my handsome dad return fifteen minutes later transformed into an old man clutching a bloody handkerchief.

But somewhere under the permafrost of post-war Britain, change was taking root. It was the depths of the Cold War, but barely an echo reached me of the momentous events which were reshaping the world. I do not recall even being aware of Mao's revolution in China, the Soviet Union's atomic bomb or the defection of Burgess and Maclean. James Bond launched his super spy career in books un-noted by me. The borders of my world were Market Balcony and the routines of school.

My social whirl was defined by a local church youth club. In a dusty hall, I met up with other callow teenagers to go through the motions of table tennis and badminton while ogling the girls. Occasionally the club held a dance, but I was stuck on the sidelines with the other non-dancers. For a while I tried to learn ballroom dancing on Sunday afternoons in the arms of a plump and sweating man with grey shoes. In an empty room over a shop, we clumped around to the strict-tempo records of Victor Silvester and his ballroom orchestra, chanting, 'Slow-slow-quick-quick-slow.' It didn't seem to bring the prospect of one of those unreachable girls any closer, and I soon gave up.

Despite their raffish former life on the road, my parents were both kindly and teetotal, undramatic and hardworking, disinclined to take holidays. My mother had played the piano in church as a girl, and she still enjoyed rolling out Ivor Novello favourites on the upright in our living-room, decorating 'We'll Gather Lilacs' with a fine flourish. I cannot recall ever hearing my father play music for pleasure. He had abandoned a solid printing apprenticeship in the jazz age for the wild insecurities of life as a freelance musician – a gesture so daring I struggle to connect it with the man I knew. He once told me tipsy toffs sometimes stuffed five-pound notes into his saxophone as they danced by. Yet he never spoke with much affection of those bohemian years which had taken him to a string of Grand Hotels, to Paris – and once to Hitler's Germany.

The only evidence that my father had lived that life

came on Sunday evenings, me in my sensible pyjamas stealing a few extra minutes before bed. It became a family ritual that my father would switch on the radio to hear the BBC Home Service announcer saying: 'And now we take you into the Palm Court of Grand Hotel, where Tom Jenkins and his orchestra are already playing for the guests.' My father had known Tom Jenkins, and shared violin lessons with him when they were teenagers in Leeds. The *Grand Hotel* selection of light classics and favourite musical comedies like *The Vagabond King* sometimes stirred him to hum along. I watched him miming a tricky passage on an imaginary violin a couple of times. But when it was over, I only remember him gently regretting the fact that most of his fellow musicians were unreliable boozers.

The perils of alcohol were a repeated theme in my parents' stories. Their disapproval of pubs and the people who went to pubs never went as far as Temperance lectures, but I was left in no doubt about their views on the demon drink. Market Street, where we lived, was bracketed by a pub at each end of the block, the Wheatsheaf and the Royal Oak. Perhaps it was because my mum's father had died an alcoholic that she always had the feeling we were in risky territory, marooned amid the drinkers.

My dad's father had been a Methodist preacher. The religious gene appeared to have failed to reach my father as comprehensively as his musical skills had eluded me. But although he seemed entirely free of spiritual feelings, he had never lost the impulse to shoulder other people's burdens. I once came in late on a wet night from some outing with schoolmates and mentioned that one of my friends was walking home. My father jumped out of bed, got dressed, and insisted on pursuing the friend in his car to give him a lift home.

My mother, another long-lapsed Methodist, used to quote, not without grudging relish, her grandmother's thunderous judgement at her girlhood mealtimes: 'For shame wanting butter on your bread!' I filed that with my father's favourite curmudgeonly Yorkshire motto: 'Them that doesn't ask, doesn't want. Them that asks are greedy.' Not that my father was a traditional stingy Yorkshireman. He was always appearing with huge bags of boiled sweets, and the only advice I ever remember him giving me was: 'Never buy cheap paint!'

For years my parents maintained a repeating dialogue, light-hearted it seemed, but sometimes, I felt, with painful undertones. My mother would sigh about the frustrations of shop life and the ugliness of Halifax. 'There's no beauty here!' she'd say with a dismissive sweep of the hand which embraced the horsemeat shop across the street and the scruffy pub on the corner. 'What do you mean – this *is* beautiful,' my father would counter with an unassailable cheeriness.

Just once, I heard it get more serious. On a sweltering summer afternoon when the tar on the street squelched under the tyres of passing buses, I was refining my spin bowling on Market Balcony, targeting three sticks propped against the wall. Suddenly I heard raised voices through an open window. I bowled again, the unwilling spy. 'It's never enough,' my father said, 'whatever I do.' The voices subsided, and I went on bowling.

I worked hard at school, finishing near the top of my class. Only *The Goon Show* on my bulky new transistor radio, smuggled under the bedsheets, hinted at a less orderly life – that, and the modern jazz from America gleaned from the record shop. Gerry Mulligan, Chet Baker and the creamy sounds of the West Coast became an instant passion. The promise of palm trees and tailfins and a cool life in the sun on the other side of the planet felt like the ultimate antidote to Market Balcony.

IT WAS A TOTAL surprise when my English teacher suggested I might apply for Cambridge. My unfocused university ambitions had been directed towards Leeds or Sheffield, and Cambridge seemed as remote as California. More out of duty than expectation, I sent off letters of application to a couple of colleges. To my mounting unease, I was invited to go down for a weekend, have interviews and stay in college. Those few days in Cambridge were my introduction to a version of life I had only read about, in stories about public schoolboys with their mysterious dormitories and secret societies and strange slang. Dining by candlelight in the Elizabethan gloom of the college hall, I met my fellow candidates. The fearsomely self-confident boy next to me began talking about the poetry he was writing, 'in the style of T.S. Eliot', he confided. Other well-modulated voices down the table chipped in, and it was clear that I was the only grammar school boy. I felt a long way from home.

I had one interview with a bearded professor who asked me to talk about the implications of the typewriter. I mumbled something banal; the prof suggested typewriters meant that only secretaries knew how to spell. Then I had a talk with another professor, young and humorous, who seemed thrilled to hear that my father had once played with Sid Seymour and his Mad Hatters. I was unsure what any of this had to do with reading English at Cambridge, but I had a glimpse of a life full of unguessed possibilities. Nothing in Glasgow or Halifax had prepared me for the magic of Cambridge in autumn. Sitting by the river, I witnessed a greeting between a couple of blokes in passing punts. 'Hi there, Clovis!' yelled one young blade. 'Hi there, Endymion,' his floppy-haired chum replied. I wondered what three years alongside the Endymions and Clovises would do to me. It seemed unlikely, and I headed home without expectations.

I still have the letter which announced my escape from Market Balcony. It is tattered now, and the typing has faded, but the message retains something of its original thrill for me. Headed 'SELWYN COLLEGE CAMBRIDGE' and dated 19 December 1955, it says: 'I am glad to be able to offer you admission to Selwyn in 1958 to read English.' It was of course a wonderful Christmas present. But I was all too aware of that yawning space before 1958, and how it would be filled – by the inescapable ordeal of military service.

2

'I'LL TEAR YOUR arm off and hit you with the soggy end!' The furious red face an inch from mine left me in no doubt that its owner could easily do that – and much more.

The drill instructor's rage was directed at my continued tendency to march like a broken doll, arms swinging mechanically without reference to legs, rhythm dislocated from the rest of the squad. The heavy rifle chafed my shoulder with every step. The burnished drill corporal was exploding yet again. This would go on, I knew, for ever.

Basic training lasted just two and a half months, but it overturned everything I knew or had imagined. I know mine must have been a pretty routine experience, shared by millions of other young men at the time. But for me, it was a crash course in reality. I felt as though I had been parachuted into a strange, hostile country without maps or guidebooks.

It began at RAF Cardington in the flatlands of Bedfordshire. In a dream, I joined the queues of young men loading up with the piles of clothing and equipment which would initiate the process of transforming us into 'airmen'. Boots, belts, uniforms, caps and kitbags were doled out, ferocious haircuts were administered.

Far more disorienting for me were my fellow conscripts. I had never encountered people like these, infinitely more strange and a lot more alarming than those gilded youths I had come upon in Cambridge. Trevor from Liverpool, decorated with fearsome tattoos, glowered at everyone who came into his orbit. I tried to merge into my blanket. Bob told me he was a bus conductor from Birmingham, and then roamed the billet scavenging for cigarettes. A manic youth called Jim jumped on to his bed and yelled, 'Let's have bloody Luxembourg!' He punched a radio on a shelf, and suddenly the room was bombarded with the uproar of 'Radio 208'. Bill Haley's thumping din was interrupted by a commercial blasting out the good news that some genius in Bristol could tell us how to win a million pounds on the Pools. The BBC Home Service I'd grown up with, and the cultured voices of Uncle Mac and Alvar Lidell, were already a distant memory. A red-headed youth across the aisle went though the motions of having vigorous sex with his mattress, and moaned loudly about what he should have been doing to his girl back in Luton at that very moment. A couple of lads were having a farting contest.

On those first evenings in the billet, I found myself amid young men who had been raised outside the evasive codes and understated manners which had shaped my life up to then – the ways, I suppose, of the English lower-middle-class. 'You can't beat a good hand wank!'

a lad with a big face and a broad West Country accent advised the billet. These were people, I discovered, who could insert 'fuck' between syllables. 'Abso-fucking-lutely!' I was stunned. I wanted to go home.

I found myself hypnotized by a ritual being pursued on the bed next to mine. A pale youth was caressing a new boot. He heated a spoon with his cigarette lighter, and then ironed the pimpled toecap. He spat on his handiwork and smoothed in layers of polish with obsessive circular motions. As I watched, the toecap began to gleam. I had barely polished my shoes at home. How would I ever replicate this alchemy?

We were lined up outside a hut, and ordered to drop our trousers. A brisk medical sergeant announced that we would now undergo 'an FFI inspection – for you sprogs, that's Freedom From Infection!' This involved offering our assorted tackle to the unenthusiastic appraisal of the sergeant, and a medical orderly who looked about fourteen. Finally, we were instructed to parcel up the civilian clothes we had arrived in just days before, and address them to home. I felt I was saying goodbye to everything I knew.

At the end of the week, the soft stuff was over and they came to get us. It was raining as the pack descended – screaming, immaculate men with brasses shining, razor creases in their trousers, hounding the recruits like bewildered cattle. In my confusion, I found myself fumbling to fold a bedsheet on the soaked parade ground. 'What the fuck's the matter with you?' a circling raptor yelled at me. 'You're looking for trouble!'

The long train journey to the basic training camp at

RAF West Kirby on the Wirral was very quiet. Even my undentable fellow recruits seemed stunned by the ferocious assault of the early morning round-up. It was only an introduction. We were yelled out of lorries, bawled up and down sheds, and at last bullied into billets. A scary little corporal shouted at us for a while as we quaked beside our iron bedframes and plywood lockers. 'Right, outside in one minute for drill!' he shrieked, and turned on his very shiny heel.

Those weeks in July and August of 1956 stick to my imagination with the ghastly intensity of a nightmare which won't let you go. The sun blitzed us as we stamped across parade grounds, the crazed tyrannies of 'bull' ruled our lives from reveille to lights out. In a daze, I learned how to construct rigid cubes out of my socks and bed sheets, reinforced with cardboard so as to survive the potty regimes of daily kit inspection. Tiny demented tasks became all-important, and I polished the insides of the lace-holes in my boots with a watch-maker's dedication. I rubbed away at the brass of my cap badge until the RAF eagle lost its feathers. The acrid smell of Brasso still puts me back in that billet, polishing desperately with my comrades in arms. Fearful of offending the short-hair gauleiters, for six weeks I avoided washing my hair and risking the suspicion of fluffiness. Eventually a camp doctor insisted on a vigorous shampoo.

Amid the madness, there were curious islands of English convention. In a slot on the front of my locker, I was required to insert a card stating my religion. Not having any clear idea what that might be, I copied the card on the locker next to mine and wrote 'C of E'. That unjustified claim consigned me to interminable church parades every Sunday. The curious cocktail of saccharine hymns, prayers and sermons stirred with a twist of sour military regulation did nothing to inspire my religious intoxication. But at least it meant that for an hour or two, I wasn't being drilled or shouted at.

Of course it was sometimes very funny – though the daily doses of animal terror rather damped down my ability to relish the moments of black comedy. An over-zealous recruit anointed the toecaps of his boots with blazing polish and then saw them fly off after a particu-larly snappy 'Atten-shun!' Another fanatic tried to secure the creases in his trousers by the application of an adhesive and found the spaces for his legs reduced to the diameter of drinking straws. All the recruits fought a daily battle against bromide, and the universal belief that RAF tea was laced with an anti-aphrodisiac to keep our youthful impulses under control. In the end, even the proudest stud had to come to terms with the impossible dilemmas of raging thirst and potential emasculation.

For all the pressures to conform, Dennis was deter-mined to hang on to something of his Teddy Boy style. This was a challenge, given the tireless attentions of the drill gauleiters. Dennis liked to spend spare moments with hand mirror, Brylcreem and comb, building a mini quiff he could hide inside his beret. Then he decided to concentrate his efforts on his peaked hat. As issued by the RAF, the 'Hat, Best Blue, peaked, Other Ranks for the use of' was not a glamorous item. Mine rested on my ears like a dustbin lid. Dennis had in mind something more raffish. He had a photo of American airmen, flaunting their hats with a style that owed more to Marlon Brando than a Marshal of the Royal Air Force. What was needed, he felt, was a little surgery. He sliced through the internal supports of the hat, and then propped up the peak with a stick. It looked pretty good, we all thought. His downfall came a few days later when he was on guard duty. Flinging a smart salute for the inspecting officer, he hit the hat and snapped the stick. The peak collapsed and the hat slumped over his eyes. His sentence for desecrating Her Majesty's property was a week of nonstop lavatory duty with menaces.

Then there was the sparrow's funeral. Returning from a crazed morning's exertions – sticking bayonets into straw dummies – we found a dead bird outside the hut. Our vast flight sergeant – 'He eats a ton and shits a ton,' said one of his corporals admiringly – was moved to the verge of tears. My entire squad, still panting from massacre practice, was ordered to doff our berets and bow our heads as the flight sergeant buried the sparrow with full military honours.

The baroque routines of 'square-bashing' quickly became the inevitable patterns of my life. I couldn't remember a time before this, or imagine it would ever end. Hauled out of bed at 6 a.m., there was just time to run for a cold water wash before rebuilding once again the psychotic layout of my bedding, socks, cleaning equipment, mug and cutlery. It would probably be trashed by the inspecting officer anyway. The mass polishing of the sacred linoleum floor was followed by the march to the cookhouse for breakfast, mug and 'eating irons' clutched in regulation order behind the back. Breakfast 'at the double' was usually grey and unidentifiable, gulped down with bromide-laced tea. Instantly, I formed a lifelong aversion to tinned tomatoes. Then it was a quick march back to the billet for another day of drill and arms drill and shouting.

I did learn some basic life skills. I darned socks, and struggled to put a crease in trousers as thick as blankets. I polished windows with screwed-up newspaper. I scrambled up walls and teetered over muddy ditches on the assault course. I became fitter than ever before, or after, in my life. I wrote letters amid the evening uproar of Radio Luxembourg and shouted curses. I survived. I counted the days.

My lifelong horror of guns was sealed on the rifle range. Stunned by the din of my .303, I failed repeatedly to make any impression on the target. After three attempts, to the increasing exasperation of the arms instructor, my target remained virgin. This was no small matter. I knew that failure to qualify with the rifle could mean I had to start the whole of basic training again – a truly numbing prospect. Driven to desperation, I took a wild risk. In the queue to deliver my target for inspection, I stabbed holes in the thing with my bayonet and passed them off as bullet marks. To this day, I wonder how I got away with it. Maybe it was just the exhaustion of an arms instructor desperate to see the back of me.

We were herded into a darkened room and ordered to watch a horror film. In lurid colour and ghastly close-up, evidence of sin and venereal disease were paraded before us. Sin looked painful. I closed my eyes through most of it, and fell into an exhausted sleep.

UNDER THE DAILY oddities of that summer of basic training, there was genuine fear. The two corporals who ruled our lives had their distinctive brands of sadism. Corporal Brownlow, a lanky and sardonic Geordie, had an unpredictable temper and a vicious ability to identify a vulnerable individual. 'You're so fucking ugly,' he snarled at a bespectacled and quivering lad. 'My God, you're ugly – I fucking hate you.' Brownlow seemed genuinely enraged by our failure to get to grips with the daft routines of arms drill. 'Why cannot you do it?' he yelled.

Corporal Smith scared me more, though. A handsome, compact cockney, even at the end of a merciless grilling, he somehow preserved the inhuman smartness of a Nazi dandy. He usually smiled as he delivered his tirades. There was no hint of Brownlow's flashes of gallows wit.

The two corporals pursued the tormenting of their raw recruits with the single-minded determination of predatory hyenas. Beds were overturned, mugs suspected of uncleanness were smashed, alleged weaknesses were targeted. Even the toughest of my comrades dreaded the moment when one of the corporals slammed into our hut. 'Corporal present!' we were required to yell, scrambling to rigid attention like a pack of Pavlovian dogs.

Mostly, Brownlow and Smith traded in threats and insults. But sometimes the menacing went further. A stubbled recruit was ordered to shave until his face was a mask of blood. When he protested that he might commit suicide, one of the corporals offered to lend him a new razor. In fact, there were several suicide attempts in the camp. We heard that a desperate young man in another part of the camp actually succeeded in hanging himself one night while the rest of us were polishing floors and cleaning lavatories. There was a terrible quietness as we paraded outside the hut next morning.

I spent my nineteenth birthday crawling across the floor of a shed attempting to get to grips with the mysteries of unblocking a jammed bren-gun in a hurry. 'Too fucking slow – do it again!' the instructor raved. In fact I only remembered it was my birthday as I was toppling into slumber after a long evening of burnishing the hut ahead of an especially rigorous inspection.

As the weeks piled up, there were hints of a saner life to come. I was summoned to an interrogation by the sleek young officer who ruled my section. As I was marched into his presence, I had a moment to review my first real toff. The well-fed face, smooth as a kid glove, was furnished with a rosebud mouth pursed in a complacent smirk. Years later, I saw a portrait of Bonnie Prince Charlie, and realized where I had seen that face before.

'Tell me about yourself,' the officer demanded languorously. I stumbled out my brief story, including for some reason my enthusiasm for modern jazz. He looked disappointed. 'And was your school in the Headmasters' Conference?' he asked. I had no idea what this meant, but I realized my bewilderment was not the right answer.

It dawned on me that I was being checked out as potential officer material. My Cambridge entry had somehow registered with the culling system, perhaps hardly surprising, as I had been told only a handful of us in my intake of 240 youths had any O-levels. But my lack of public school credentials and hopeless military performance were clearly closing the door to officer status. 'Perhaps something in intelligence,' the officer murmured, but his attention was already wandering as I was marched out.

As I crawled towards my reprieve from basic training, the omens for my military career did not look promising. I seemed to be out of step on and off the parade ground. Mistaking my hopeless shamblings during arms drill for willful insubordination, Corporal Brownlow pulled me out of the squad. 'You know your problem?' he yelled. 'You've got a fucking superior complex!' At that moment, this was very far from being true.

Then I had a letter from my first real girfriend back in Halifax to say she had found someone else. My fumbled affair with Jennifer had been conducted over my final months at school, in bus shelters and in occasional trysts on a Pennine hillside. In those repressed times when lust did unequal battle with fear, we praised ourselves for 'not going too far'. Now, Jennifer's letter told me she had fallen for Fred. It seemed he had won her heart with his talents as a boogie-woogie pianist. I reflected with bitterness that from what I knew of him I doubted whether Fred would have maintained the self-denying regime of his predecessor. In a flush of Byronic despair, I lay on my cast-iron bed amid the uproar of the evening's floor polishing and wrote a poem which began: 'My heart's an empty ballroom, after the dancers have fled . . .'

I fixed my sights obsessively on the end of basic training. There seemed no point in fretting about what might come after, since my future was clearly in the hands of the smirking officer and the shadowy powers who ruled him.

In the final days of square-bashing, the people who had tyrannized us for ten awful weeks suddenly organized a day out. We were led off to the dismal resort of New Brighton on the muddy banks of the Mersey. Corporals Brownlow and Smith laid on a ghoulish parody of 'joining the lads' and insisted on paying for us to go on funfair rides. Hideously conspicuous in our 'Best Blue' dress uniforms, we wandered amid the holiday-makers like a reluctant troop of Boy Scouts on a compulsory ramble. I almost yearned for the smell of Brasso to obliterate the cloying stench of candyfloss. Most of us couldn't wait to go back to camp. And of course the next morning, the corporals were back on their best feral form.

A few days later, we were assembled to hear our fates for the next two years. Sweat soaked through my stiff new shirt as I shuffled in the queue of conscripts towards the pressed and shining sergeant who would deliver my future. Would it be 'cook' or 'clerk' or, God help me, something to do with guns? At last it was my turn. The sergeant thrust his mouth at my ear. 'Russian Linguist,' he rasped.

Those words broke the malign spell which seemed to

have invaded my life in that summer of 1956. I had no idea what it would mean, but it was the moment when 'Aircraftman Second Class Woodhead L. J.' became a footsoldier in the espionage battalions.

3

My LIFE AS A COG in the spy machine had a confusing start. As so often in the months to come, I found myself propelled in bewildering directions by forces I could neither identify nor understand. I am pretty sure it had more to do with misplaced bits of paper in dingy offices than with the devious strategies of the Cold War.

After a precious few days at home, trying to shrug off an instinct to march rather than walk round the house, I was ordered to report to RAF West Malling, a former Battle of Britain airfield in Kent. Schooled in the alarming barminess of basic training, it was hard to adjust to the soggy routines of an RAF camp in peacetime. On my first morning, a corporal slouched into the billet and I had to stifle my instinct to bawl out the ingrained acknowledgement. No one even looked up. Instead of square-bashing's theatres of humiliation, parades at West Malling were a somnolent shambles. A rumpled sergeant rallied his forces with the command, 'Fall in, hairy arses!' After a few days, I began to know the awful tedium of National Service life. Day followed featureless day, with nothing to give shape or purpose.

RAF West Malling had an eventful history. Spitfires had flown from the airfield to shoot down Nazi doodle-bugs; Dambuster hero Guy Gibson had been based there. Three lost German Fokker 190s had landed there in error in 1943. The dashing Captain Peter Townsend, doomed lover of Princess Margaret who had declared the end of their affair just before I began National Service, had done a stint at West Malling. The place even claimed a ghost, a spectral figure in World War II flying gear who was said to wander round, peering through windows. Now I felt like that ghost, lost and drifting.

No one at West Malling had ever heard of any Russian course, and they plainly didn't know what to do with me. For weeks I was moved around from haul-ing dustbins on the camp rubbish truck to shifting furniture. I was recruited to a squad picking up rocks in a field. I struggled to stay awake during long nights of guard duty, armed with a pickaxe handle. I read the entire works of Jane Austen on my bunk, in an effort to break out into an alternative universe. The most dramatic incident in my empty days was being ticked off by the camp commander for walking across a for-bidden patch of grass. The gathering crisis over Suez was a rumour from a distant star. I began to wonder if the Russian Linguist assignment might be military code for a life as an odd-job man.

Like most of my RAF postings to come, West Malling was about as far away from Halifax and home as could be devised by some hard-hearted pen-pusher with a malicious sense of humour. I made the tortuous journey a couple of times – walking, then busing, then local train, then main-line train, then all the way back – and finally gave up. I decided to dip my toe into London instead. Those Saturdays in the big city were an adventure.

I had been to London only once before, on a thrilling three-day expedition with my parents to visit the Festival of Britain in 1951. We had travelled south all night on a clattering steam train, and my first sight of the capital was the back streets of Bloomsbury as my father scurried around trying to find a hotel for his bleary family. He quickly discovered that the draw of the Festival, with its promise of a brave new post-war world, had jammed every small guest house for miles around. We ended up in the faded grandeur of the Russell Hotel. It was by far the most splendid building I had ever seen, with a sweeping staircase which seemed to have been borrowed from one of those musicals I had seen at the Halifax Regal. Even in my exhaustion I was aware that my parents were fretting about the cost. We moved out the next day for a humbler refuge.

The Festival site on the South Bank was a wonder. For a wide-eyed teenager with sci-fi enthusiasms, the Skylon and the Dome of Discovery and 3D cinema and all the gadgets of the new 'age of optimism' were irresistible. We went out to the new Heathrow Airport to marvel at the half-dozen passenger airliners, deafened by the roar of their propellers. I came home, convinced that London was a miraculous nirvana.

Wandering around Soho in the rain with my paka-mac on Saturday trips from West Malling, things looked less glamorous. But it still felt exciting to be alone in London. I sampled bookshops and museums and ventured into Lyons Corner House Café for egg and chips. Best of all, I found my way to a jazz club in a little basement in Chinatown. The dazzling tenor sax of a young Tubby Hayes held me enthralled until I had to dash for the last train back to Kent. Hiking back to camp along darkened lanes, the spell was only broken when I arrived at the guardroom gates. Another week on the rubbish truck loomed.

Then at last, in early November 1956, I was told that the vital document had arrived. I was to report immediately to RAF Ruislip, at the outer limits of the Central Line. After slogging my kitbag from the underground station to the camp gates, I was greeted with incomprehension. 'What the hell are you doing here?' spluttered the duty corporal. 'You should be in Scotland!'

On the platform of King's Cross station, where the smog tangled with the sour smoke of grimy steam locomotives, I met up at last with the Joint Services School for Linguists – or at least with evidence that it actually existed. Huddled together with their kitbags were several dozen airmen, looking as lost as I felt. Conversation struggled against the hubbub of the station, but I gathered that we were all headed for the same place – JSSL Crail. We piled into the carriages for the overnight journey north.

It was a cheerier and more hopeful train than the fearful transport which had hauled me off to basic training four months before. The hours in the darkness up over the shoulder of England towards the border were filled with excited chatter about what might happen next. My fellow Linguists were a bright bunch, most of them like me marking time before university, all of them reassuringly unmilitary. Trousers looked baggy, brasses were dull. No one seemed to have much of an idea about what awaited us.

We were joining the Cold War at a dangerous moment. As we rumbled through the darkness that night, Soviet tanks were smashing an anti-communist uprising in Hungary, signalling a nightmarish new escalation in the superpower confrontation. Tens of thousands had been killed, and there were fears of world war. The Joint Services Russian course had already been denounced at the UN by the Soviet Ambassador Andrei Vyshinsky as a 'Spy School'. It was not a time when government or military were inclined to share their plans for combating the Red Peril with a mob of junior National Servicemen. One of my new colleagues told me that when he'd been accepted for the Russian course, his neighbours had been quizzed about his background by strange men in macs. If the mysterious men had ever visited Market Balcony, they must have had a frustrating time. Still, the suggestion that some of us had merited a security vetting, and the fact that we were now headed for a remote spot on the map somewhere in Scotland, seemed to confirm the secrecy of our mission.

As it got light, our train dawdled through a succession of tiny Fife villages with exotic names: Kinghorn, Dysart, Largo, Elie, Pittenweem. It was a litany which was to become the utterly familiar sequence of stepping-stones for our comings and goings over the months to come. Then, at the end of everything, we pulled into Crail.

Bouncing along the single main street in the back of a lorry, I had a first sight of the ancient fishing village which was to be my home base for the next seven months. Spiky trees patrolled the street, guarding sober grey stone houses. There was not a human being to be seen. Beyond the village, the road sliced straight between fields drained of colour. A pewter sea lined the horizon. A dank grey mist rolled to meet us, and the cold seeped through our stiff greatcoats. Then, like a black and white photo emerging from the developing dish, low huts began to take shape behind a barbed-wire fence. 'I suppose that's it,' someone said. 'Looks a bit like Stalag Luft 11.'

We clambered down from the truck on a raw November morning to a first view of JSSL Crail. It was not an uplifting prospect. A few weary-looking huts squatted on the scrubby grass, a concrete road sloped up towards more huts on the top of a hill. A few sea-gulls squawked. But at least the military welcoming party seemed devoid of menace. Even the formidable-looking figure with a red sash who declared that he was 'Corporal of the Horse Charnley' seemed more like an uncle than a tyrant. A handful of dejected-looking NCOs delivered a few basic orders, and we tramped off up the hill towards our billets for the first of the hundreds of ascents which would shape our lives for months to come.

A high proportion of the JSSL recruits were grammar school boys, many like me from the North of England.

We were, it occurs to me now, the shambling reconnaissance patrol for a social revolution which, in the next decade, would grab Britain by the scruff of the neck. I had read somewhere this was the era of the Angry Young Men, and though I couldn't detect much evidence of seditious rage among my sleepy comrades that morning, as 'Aircraftmen Second Class' we were the innocent invaders of a bastion of British privilege long occupied by our betters. Espionage, after all, was a posh business. Spies were traditionally cultivated in Oxbridge, and understood the codes of the ruling class. 'You might potter about, old boy, and take the odd snap ... .' Now, it seemed, the riff-raff were at the gates.

JSSL Crail was the third location for the Russian Linguist course. Established in a hurry in September 1951, two schools had been scrambled into down-at-heel camps in Surrey and Cornwall. Not long before I arrived, desks, blackboards and teachers had been transported 400 miles north to the Fife coast as the trawl of trainee Linguists expanded to recruit hundreds of fresh-faced National Servicemen.

Once we had puffed our way to the top of the hill, the camp looked slightly less bleak. There was an impressive view now of the North Sea, and of a craggy-looking island on the horizon. Over the months ahead, it was to become the daily backdrop as I shivered or sweltered on the parade ground in the half-hearted service ritual which preceded another day's immersion in the language of our Cold War enemy.

Suddenly, there seemed to be a lot of activity. Young men in assorted uniforms, canvas haversacks over their shoulders, were pouring out of huts. It was my first indication that JSSL might be more than a little experiment in a forgotten backwater. Soon, there were scores of youths heading for the parade ground, spruce-looking army blokes burdened with webbing, junior airmen trying to look like civilians, and louche navy types ambling past as though on the way to their London clubs.

I was joining a battalion of 700 Russian Linguists at JSSL that day. It became clear that the reason for my months in limbo since basic training was that I had been put in storage until the start of a new intake, joining a production line which delivered a fresh batch of 'translator entries' four times a year. Marching down the hill again after dumping our kitbags in billets which seemed, miraculously, to have some kind of heating, it was already apparent that I was about to be involved in serious business.

We were given an opening pep talk by the camp principal, a no-nonsense Brigadier. Assembled in a cavernous building which appeared to double as a cinema and a gymnasium, the newcomers were abruptly advised that this was not going to be a soft touch. We would work. We would work hard. Although we were studying Russian, we would not neglect our military training. He concluded with a time-honoured military mantra: 'You play ball with me, and I'll play ball with you. But remember,' he added, 'it's my ball.'

We were marched across the main road to the lower camp, where we were told we would be issued with the tools of our new trade. This curious layout, with the living billets bisected from the classrooms by a public road, came to feel like a metaphor for the essential schizophrenia of JSSL. In a previous life the camp had been HMS *Jackdaw*, a naval torpedo training station, and the military back-story had seeped into the fabric of the place. You half expected to come upon John Mills and a teenage Richard Attenborough doing something brave with an unexploded weapon. Now it had been transformed into a crammer school, inhabited by swotty young men, many peering at this odd outpost through thick spectacles, plainly ill-equipped to deal with anything more menacing than a vocabulary list.

It was a split personality which was to run through my life in the months to come. But slugging back up the hill that first evening, my knapsack laden with my 'Semyonova Grammar' and my reading primer, the numbingly titled *Ordinary People*, JSSL Crail certainly did not feel much like that glamorous 'spy school'.

4

I FLICKED MY TONGUE along my palate in a desperate attempt to locate the right sound. For all the long-suffering efforts of Mr Danilochkin, I struggled to hear the difference between a hard and a soft Russian 'L'. The coke stove had turned the little classroom into a sauna, and I was sweating. My classmates shifted on their hard chairs, bored by my slow progress in the foothills of the Russian language. Private MacFeet, a fierce little army Linguist with hair like a fox's brush, let out a low groan.

Those first weeks of struggling to get a grip on the elusive fundamentals of a strange new language were for me as tough as basic training. From the very beginning, classes were almost entirely conducted in Russian. On the first morning, an elderly man with a face reminiscent of Nikita Khrushchev held up a pencil and said: '*Eta karandash!*' It seemed a humble start to our careers in espionage, but within minutes it became a lot more demanding.

For the moment, though, I was still catching up with the reality of being here, part of an adventure I could never have anticipated. The noise of the language was instantly seductive, the looping, caressing vowel sounds curling round our heads like cigarette smoke. The teachers were an exotic tribe: Russian, Polish, Latvian, Ukrainian, Lithuanian, Czech, émigrés in flight from the varied craziness of the Soviet Empire. They included the odd prince, an occasional baron, a couple of counts, assorted diplomats and army officers.

Mr Scobie had been deported to Siberia in a cattle truck, and still looked traumatized by the experience. Colonel Bystram told us he used to go hunting with the Tsar. Mr Koshevnikov, regal and highly strung, was never seen without his dog. Tiny, irascible Mr Sternberg had once been in the SS.

Rounded up for a group photograph, they looked an odd bunch – as though a scatter of refugees fleeing from a bombed-out academy somewhere in war-ravaged Europe had been kitted out in cast-offs from a travelling rep company. In the photo, louche trilbys line up with raffish berets, duffel coats stand shoulder to shoulder with macs which look as if they've been borrowed from some *film noir*. One of my future instructors sports dark glasses and a bow tie. Another tips his hat with a smile which suggests that this is just one more episode in a life rich in absurdities.

Some of the staff were clearly as dislocated as their pupils by finding themselves in this odd place on the edge of Scotland. They were paid a paltry £400 per year, which even in 1950s Fife was barely a subsistence wage. While single instructors lived on the camp, teachers with families had to find rented accommodation in the surrounding villages. One lamented that he had to light his room with a candle to save electricity. Few were real teachers, and many spoke limited English. Most of them were kindly enough, and patient beyond reason with the squads of young men they were required to instruct in the language they had left behind.

To be sure, my early fumblings with Russian were not the fault of the teachers. At first contact, the elaborate and unpredictable rules and structures of the language seemed designed to defeat outsiders. The alphabet was strange enough, though my O-level Greek gave me some kind of start in getting to grips with letters dreamed up by St Cyril to echo Greek Christian ideas.

To compound the tangles with my tongue and the battles with those hard and soft letters, I soon found myself floundering in the labyrinth of a language which made the contortions of Latin and Greek seem like the simple mumblings of Bill and Ben the Flowerpot Men on toddlers' TV. Russian nouns shifted according to fluid rules, verbs shimmered around under a haze of moods and mysteries. There were no words for 'the' or 'a' or 'I am'. And what could I make of a language which changed the endings of words depending on whether you were talking about one thing, or up to four things, or more than four things?

I still have some of the teaching booklets which defined my life over those months. God knows why I kept them for more than four decades, hauled between attics and sheds in a succession of houses. Somehow they felt as impossible to throw out as those awful snaps

of forgotten holidays and half-remembered acquaintances. It occurs to me now that if the authorities had
been tipped off about my strange hoard, it could have
provoked a visit from the men in macs.

Headed 'Basic Russian Course', they were typed out
and copied on to white and green and pink sheets and
stapled together. Musty now and fraying, the staples
rusting, they chart my uncertain progress towards acquir-
ing the tools of my new trade.

IN WEEK THREE, we grappled with 'Monosyllabic
Verbs', and were advised of 'the rule concerning sibilants
and gutturals'. To lighten the spartan lists of conjuga-
tions and vocabulary, there were 'Oral-Aural Drills',
little dramas of Russian life. 'Does your wife often wash
the floor?' asks some nosy interrogator. 'No, not often.'
'Does your wife sing as she works?' the questioner per-
sists, clearly a Commissar of Positive Thought. 'No, she
doesn't like singing,' is the bleak reply.

By week six, we met 'The Dative Case', and the cosy
dialogues featured 'House repairs', 'A bookshop' and 'At
the post office'. There was only the merest hint of our
military purpose with occasional phrases like 'He was
killed at the front'. As the weeks piled up, the mood of
the teaching booklets darkened.

The JSSL routines were gruelling. At 8 a.m. sharp
we were lined up for the inevitable parade, and the
sparse military personnel had their moment to try to
impose some semblance of service discipline. Plainly,
confronted by several hundred lost causes, their hearts
weren't really in it. Most of us were still half asleep

anyway. By 8.15 a.m., we were marching down the hill to the teaching compound. We were immediately in the thick of it. Grammar drill was followed by Russian reading, English/Russian translation moved on to Russian/English translation. We marched from Russian dictation to a lecture in Russian. Then there was another hour of Russian/English translation, and finally a volley of thirty new words to send us back up the hill to our billets and an evening of homework and vocabulary polishing.

Slowly, inexorably, the blizzard of Russian began to envelop me. The JSSL policy was 'immersion', and we were duly immersed. The lovely sound of it seeped into us, and we began to chatter in Russian. English words started to blur. Steeped now in the Russian alphabet, those Cyrillic letters which looked deceptively familiar, H, P, C, B, invaded our reading of English with their Russian equivalents – N, R, S, and V. Familiar signs and notices seemed to be sending coded messages – the local Co-op appeared to us to have been re-labelled as a forbidding Soviet outpost – 'Soor'.

As the instructors became more familiar, one of them shared earthy Russian proverbs with us. Usually, they were a bit opaque. '*Ya idu kuda Tsantsar idyot pyeshkom*' literally means 'I'm going where even the rich man Tsantsar goes on foot.' This, we were advised, was a proverbial way of saying 'I'm going to the lavatory.' One Linguist retailed a very Eastern European story told to his class by one of the instructors, Mr Scobie. It concerned 'the string game'. When he was a young student in Warsaw, Scobie recalled how his friends would sit around a table outside a bar and remove the umbrella. Then they each threaded a string through the hole and tied one to end to their penis. The other ends were scrambled together on the table. Finally each young man took it in turn to choose a string and pull it hard. 'Didn't that hurt?' the class had asked. 'Only if you tugged your own string,' Scobie replied.

We handed out Russian nicknames, and John Morris became 'Strel' – derived from the Russian for 'shoot', and John's tendency to shoot the shit. I heard people murmuring Russian in their sleep.

From the stew of military drudgery and language cramming, the outlines of my fellow Linguists began to emerge. Recalling the boys who had slogged through square-bashing alongside me, this seemed to be a collection of young men from a different species.

They look back at me now from the faded black and white snaps I took over those months at JSSL. I had become a bit of a photo nut in my last year at school, slogging my Zeiss Ikon with its bellows like a miniature concertina on family holidays and youth club outings. Corralling parents and friends into stiff little groups, composing vapid 'mood' photos of rowing boats or dead leaves, I had grown attached to the rituals of the amateur photographer. In those days before auto-focus and auto-exposure, I grappled with the mysteries of 'F-stops' and 'depth of field', unsure that anything would 'come out'. The moment of opening the bag of prints on the pavement outside the chemist's shop to find that I had managed to capture smiling uncles and grey landscapes never lost its magic for me.

Quite why I was allowed to infiltrate the camera into JSSL is a puzzle. The 'Spy School' seems to have been oddly casual about security. I can't recall any serious efforts to conceal what we were doing, and the sagging fences which dribbled round the camp would have greeted any potential intruder with an Ealing comedy spoof of a secret base. We heard that the dour locals down the road in Crail called JSSL 'yon interruptors' school' and that seemed to be the limit of their interest. I still have my photo of a weary-looking Mr Danilochkin in a JSSL classroom, slumped in front of a wall chart of the Russian alphabet. Someone has drawn a funny face on the blackboard behind him. My amateur photographer's passions don't seem to have been much stirred by the drab spectacle of language-cramming. Most of my pictures are of my fellow Linguists, larking about after classes, snoozing on the grass, lined up and gazing at the camera like kids on a school outing. I have long forgotten the surnames, but I can still see the faces.

There was Charlie, who smoked a pipe and claimed to know the word for 'nutmeg grater' in forty-two languages. We challenged him for the Cherokee Indian version, and he instantly came up with something vaguely convincing. There was Robin, a gangling former Wykehamist who seemed permanently out of touch with the bewildering naughtiness of the world. Robin's wide-eyed sweetness and inability to think ill of anybody or anything protected him like a Martian force field in a 50s sci-fi film. There was Don, a lanky bespectacled Yorkshireman who was engaged to be married – an exotic rarity in a community where very few of us had girlfriends. There was Ivor, a red-faced, red-haired cockney, fittingly fiery and unquenchably energetic. Ivor was to become one of the few Linguists whose life ran parallel with my own over the rest of our National Service. There was Dave, erudite and didactic, who insisted that 'a fugue is better than a fuck'. At this point in his life, I doubted that Dave had any more information than the rest of us to make that judgement. There was Colin, untroubled by an acne so extreme it seemed like a gesture of defiance, and who elevated his gaucheness into a lifestyle. There was a spidery Welshman whom I can now only remember as 'Morgan', a youth so vaporous and mousy that his mere presence seemed to still the air around him. Morgan knelt to say his prayers on the polished lino of his bedspace every night, commanding the uneasy respect of the thirty free thinkers in the billet. I recall that just as we were falling asleep one night, the hut was bombarded by a sudden clattering uproar of unguessable origin. In the silence that followed, a voice piped up: 'It's probably Morgan, coming in pissed again.'

Those photos of mine also record something of the after-hours japes which became regular safety valves to release the pressures of our non-stop cramming. In one picture, a Linguist 'toreador' flaunts his RAF rain cape to make a pass at an improvised 'bull' – another Linguist under a bedsheet with sweeping brush horns. Intense competitions, with floor-polishing 'bumpers' as curling stones, were fought out on the gleaming linoleum of our billet. It was mostly silly and innocent, though on occasions the fooling did become more ambitious. I heard about one unfortunate who found a dead seagull in his bed, and another chap who woke up in the depths of a freezing Crail night to find that his bed had been carried into the middle of the parade ground. I shudder to think what the less decorous Army contingent, known by the RAF Linguists as 'brown jobs', might have got up to. The Navy Linguists, relaxing in their silk paisley dressing-gowns, probably borrowed their pranks from P.G. Wodehouse and Gussy Finknottle.

A couple of the bolder escapades became minor myths among Crail graduates. One involved a local scare about an escaped panther which was said to have been spotted in the fields around the camp. For a Linguist called Jim this was just too good to miss. Hearing that a fellow Linguist, Jock, was alarmed by the rumours that a wild predator was on the loose, Jim determined to bring the beast of East Neuk to JSSL. He turned his black duffel coat inside out and sewed on a pair of panther ears. Then he waited in the ceiling of a hut among the hot water pipes. When Jock returned from the NAAFI that night, Jim bounded across the roof making big-cat noises. The target was gratifyingly spooked, but the triumph was short-lived. Prowling around once too often, Jim was rumbled and unmasked.

The affair of 'Horse's hat' threatened to become more serious. Someone decided it would be fun to steal the Corporal of the Horse's remarkable headgear – a relic of his career in the Life Guards, with a peak which clamped down on the bridge of his nose. Horse was not amused. For a time, dire mass punishments were threatened, before the precious item mysteriously reappeared.

Amid all the vocabulary lists and grammar exercises, we were also invited to dip our toes into the vast ocean of Russian literature. If they had realized it was going on, I can only imagine how this would have been received by the disgruntled soldiery who were trying to grab us for extra bren-gun drill. Lounging around with our word lists was no doubt bad enough in their eyes. Poncing about with poems and plays written by old Russkies with wigs would have seemed beyond indulgence. Even for the unseen high-ups who planned the JSSL course, I wondered how these excursions into Russia's literary heritage could be justified. Maybe it was seen as some kind of consolation for our instructors, yearning after mellow evenings in a half-remembered Moscow salon.

Whatever the motives, from time to time we were introduced to poems and plays and stories by the likes of Pushkin and Lermontov. Much of it, of course, was beyond our fledgling grasp of the language, and I often laboured over a paragraph for an hour with a dictionary. But something of the electricity I had felt when I first came upon George Herbert or Gerard Manley Hopkins sparked in me again. I swooned over a succulent poem about the coming of spring, and a line stuck with me: '*Idyot, gudyot zelyoni shum*' – 'the green sound comes and goes'. Pushkin's story of demonic gambling 'The Queen of Spades', with its love-crazed prince and ghostly countess, was another favourite, after those bleak little domestic dramas in our study sheets. And of course, the inevitable result was that we were consuming yet more Russian.

We all knew that we were cramming with the threat of execution. An essential part of 'playing ball' the Crail way was the weekly test. This was the regular Darwinian ordeal through which the the fittest were checked for survival potential, and the unfit were 'returned to unit'. I found I had to work harder to keep up than I had ever done in my life. JSSL Crail was proving to be anything but the two years of sleepy drudgery I had anticipated for my National Service.

After a couple of months, we were put through a progress test. The very real threat of being cast out to a regular service life of bull and boredom was a powerful incentive, and very few people fell below the required 75 per cent pass rate. Relief and mutual congratulation abounded during those dry-mouthed scrums round the bulletin board just inside the main gate. But there was always another ingredient – competition.

We were subjected to further culling after the progress test. 'Streaming' put top students into élite classes of high flyers. I was not among the chosen, and I was aware that I was not alone in my muffled envy of the elect. It was inevitable that a collection of young men would be seeking to carve out their place in the pecking order. In a different community, it might have involved taunts and fist fights. For my bright and restless comrades, the weapons became a command of the word lists and a top score in the exams. Steve, a fresh-faced Londoner with an unquenchable wide boy's perkiness, seemed an unlikely language boffin. Many people were startled, and not a little put out, when he began to appear regularly close to the top of the weekly test scores. Nothing was said directly, of course. This was still Britain in the 1950s, and obvious displays of ambition or rivalry were not encouraged, especially among young men headed for university. Still, I suspect none of us were free of the class assumptions which had shaped our lives, and Steve's effortless ability to master the Russian which was taxing people who considered themselves his social superiors was not universally celebrated. On the other hand, no one was ever in any doubt that Oliver and Jeremy and Hugo were high flyers and would go far.

And there was always the ultimate prize. From the earliest days at Crail, we all knew that a select few of us would be chosen to study Russian at Cambridge University. The lucky ones would throw off their uniforms for a charmed life of languorous hours with Pushkin, wearing civvies, and indulging in regular punting. At least that was how it shimmered in the collective imagination as we trudged up and down the hill, pursued by swarms of qualitative adjectives and interrogative pronouns and the day's production target of another thirty new words.

Peter felt like a Cambridge cert from the beginning. Within days of spotting one another across the hut, he and I became soulmates. With a tangle of curly blond hair, a public-school self-confidence, and a voice as ripe as a young Donald Sinden's, he was an unlikely pal for me. But I quickly discovered that he was wickedly funny, and effortlessly exuded a sense, thrilling to me, that he was simply an unclaimable civilian in a silly uniform. He spotted me devouring a book which was my temporary obsession, *One-Upmanship* by Stephen Potter. For some reason, this cranky guidebook on how to upstage your friends by shameless ploys – such as inventing old war wounds – delighted both of us. 'How to make the other man feel that something has gone wrong, however slightly', Potter's theme, became our joint project. We pondered his advice on 'How to make people feel awkward about religion' and 'The art of winning Christmas games'. We tried to incorporate his hints for 'OK words', adding 'mystique' and 'classique' to our vocabulary lists. We dedicated ourselves to imitating Potter's wildly overwrought schemes, like getting off a train at the last conceivable moment with the aim of making passengers fretting in the aisles feel gauche. I don't recall that anyone even noticed.

The opportunities for one-upmanship were inevitably limited among our monastic community of Linguists in the Fife outback. Perhaps it was the sense of feeling liberated by the companionship of a confident rebel, but Peter made things seem more fun. Even the periodic attempts by the camp's dispirited military staff to instil some fighting skills into the flaccid Linguists, raising terrible echoes of basic training, felt less daunting with Peter chortling quietly alongside me. The fact that there was someone else to relish the strange commands of the arms instructor: 'You've dismantled your bren-gun – now MANTLE it again!' almost made fumbling with guns enjoyable. And although Peter was far better at it than I, the ordeal of failing to climb a rope in the gymnasium felt merely laughable rather than tormenting.

Still, life on the camp remained resolutely bleak.

Linoleum had to be burnished, and boots were never allowed to sully the sacred floors. In the huts, we slid around on blanket slippers, like shambling skaters. The food served up in the cookhouse was even more dire than the swill doled out during basic training. Watery tinned tomatoes were a signature dish. For a couple of weeks, there was even an outbreak of dysentery. An exchange with the Corporal of the Horse, reported by one RAF man, summed up the horror of mealtimes. On cookhouse duty, Horse was supposed to register any complaints about the food. The brave airman suggested that the peas were like lead shot. 'Hard, are they?' replied the Corporal, with what seemed like concern. 'They shouldn't be. They've been through me twice.' Another Linguist reported that while he was doing punishment duty in the cookhouse, he was ordered to soak piles of swedes in pineapple juice. Served up as 'pineapple chunks', they were consumed without comment. Food parcels from home were seized upon like emergency aid in a war zone. It was a surprise to no one when it was revealed that the Cook and Quartermaster had been selling our fresh produce to the locals. They both received stiff prison sentences, but I'm not sure that the food got much better.

It was brutally cold in Crail that winter of 1956/7. We often had to brace ourselves against the gales to stay upright on the parade ground. Even the stoves in the classrooms, fed with screwed-up Russian newspapers and sea coal, left us shivering. We pored over our study sheets, wrapped in thick greatcoats. One aged instructor was in the habit of draping his soggy handkerchiefs over the classroom radiator to dry. Inevitably, his students were soon sneezing along with him. Venturing down the long road to Crail was like hiking in a wind tunnel, and there was a brief fashion for lagging your legs with newspaper inside thick trousers to provide insulation against the elements.

For the locals, life in Crail was tough. Apart from the fishing, most people carved out a living from the land. Every year, children were given a month off school to work at the potato harvest, toiling alongside their parents to pick up the 'tatties' with their bare hands. The few pennies they earned were handed over to their mothers for winter clothes. The village depended heavily on the camp up the road for its living. But parents were always wary of those licentious young men who might have designs on their daughters. Many families frowned on the idea of local dances, and for them the decorous Miss Crail contest was an annual parade of sinfulness.

In the Kingdom of East Neuk, where Crail was situated, fun and frolics were thin on the ground. We were hardly equipped to paint the town red anyway, after lining up on the weekly pay parade to collect our miserly one pound two shillings and sixpence. Bolder spirits sometimes dared a muted comment about the wretched pay by improvising wildly irreverent salutes while the payment officer was distracted by his lists and money-counting. Fingers in ears and up noses provided only temporary consolation for permanent poverty.

The JSSL magazine, *Samovar*, had been born in the early days of the course, as an offshoot of a 'Russian Club' in Bodmin. The club was permitted as an alternative to Wednesday afternoon sports, and the founding of *Samovar* helped to justify the exemption from all that muddy exercise. The magazine was an odd hybrid, half in English, half in Russian, bashed out on a JSSL typewriter, duplicated and stapled together. Despite its home-made production, *Samovar* did not lack pretension. An editorial could quote 'the Greek Philosopher Lalophilus', and parodies of Chaucer rubbed shoulders with monographs on Dostoevsky and poems with titles like 'Sea Sorrow'. There was also a good deal of laboured schoolboy humour.

Samovar catches one of the few highlights on offer in the Crail area with a review of *Rock Around the Clock*, daringly screened in a local cinema. True, the review somewhat dampens the seditious potential of the film in its opening remarks: '"All arts aspire to the condition of music," said Schopenhauer . . .' But it does conclude with a rather stuffy pat on the balding head of Bill Haley: 'It is, one may note, enjoyed by Princesses as well as Edwardians' – presumably a haughty label for Teddy Boys. 'Morally,' the review concedes, 'it is no more impeachable than the Charleston. To ignore Rock 'n' Roll and its success would be to ignore the tastes and habits of the general public in every age which have done more to dictate our environment and the actual course of our lives than the works of Plato, Michelangelo or Dante.' Hardly the stuff to get them ripping up the seats of Aird's Cinema in Crail (Monday, Wednesday and Friday at 6.15 p.m.).

Samovar gives a picture of the limited opportunities for a big night out after a long day with the vocabulary list. The highlight is a production of Aristophanes' *The Clouds* ('Five Choric Odes in the Original Greek'), by the School and Ladies of St Andrews University. Home-made entertainment on the camp includes a Chopin recital and gatherings of the JSSL Bridge Club. There are plaintive pleas for new members from the Philosophy Society and the Ski Club. For those thirsting for more Russian, *Samovar* reviews a JSSL production of Pushkin's *Boris Godunov* – on a bare stage in the gym, with actors uncostumed, in Russian. The review, after regretting 'the acoustic difficulties of the gymnasium', makes it clear that there hadn't exactly been a rush on the box office: 'A criticism concerns the regimentation of part of the audience. Attendance at any form of artistic entertainment should be voluntary.'

The ads in *Samovar* provide the strongest whiff of the times. Even the lettering returns me instantly to the age of typewriters and carbon paper. 'Clothes of distinction', declares an ad for Caird and Sons, alongside a drawing of a bloke resembling a young Prince Philip with a hankie in his top pocket and a pipe in his mouth. Other ads offer 'Large selection of Roadster and Racing cycles' and 'Strads sports trousers – give you that clean cut look'. For that special night out, there's the Balcomie Links Hotel, near Crail, with 'Dominoes and Television Lounge' (Dinners by Arrangement). The Cinema House in St Andrews clearly hoped to appeal to a discerning student audience with its claim that 'every picture shown is specially selected because of its high entertainment value'.

It was with Peter that I came upon a modest outpost

of counter-culture. On the dour main street of Crail, we found the Music Box Café. It was hardly a den of reefer madness, just a sparse room with a scatter of Formica tables and chairs. But on the counter, a gleaming chromium-plated cappuccino machine gurgled and hissed. More thrilling still, they had installed a jukebox. In the sober universe of Crail, it was an alien as improbable as a flying saucer. Suddenly, the thing erupted.

I can still recall the shock of hearing Elvis Presley's 'Hound Dog' roaring through the Music Box Café that afternoon. Peter and I were instantly hooked. We hoarded our cups of stagnating coffee over dozens of replays. On grey afternoons, we trudged down the long straight road from the camp for regular fixes of Elvis and cappuccino. The arrival of 'Heartbreak Hotel' at the Music Box refuelled our obsession. I still don't really know why we were so excited by our encounters with Elvis. Since those first contacts, I've never been particularly interested in the King or in his increasingly turgid music. Maybe it was about discovering something beyond the confines of our intense little JSSL community. Sharing the faintly seditious discovery of Elvis with a kindred spirit provided a temporary escape from the routines of Russian irregular verbs and the ordeals of the gymnasium.

Our other discovery was the Bottle Dungeon. Nothing more achingly confirms the deprivations of the social wilderness that was Fife in those months than our repeated visits to the place. The pilgrimages involved a bumpy bus trip along a dozen miles of back roads to the town of St Andrews. It was, and is, a pretty spot. In the fifties, students in their scarlet gowns still decorated the quiet streets. But apart from the pleasures of high tea in a café unchanged since the days of *Brief Encounter*, there wasn't much to divert a bored young serviceman. There was the occasional Saturday evening dance at the university, a stand-off of blushing young men and women surveying one another across a divide of polished floor. But for Peter and me, nothing rivalled the allure of the Bottle Dungeon.

The ancient castle in St Andrews hangs on the edge of a cliff at the end of the town, overlooking the sea. There's not much left of it after the centuries of ghastly doings in those parts. But one wet Saturday afternoon we came upon a crypt in the furthest corner of the castle, carved out of the rockface. A flight of worn stone steps led down to a claustrophobic chamber. In the middle of the floor, there was a low circular wall. We peered over the edge into a pit. 'Here we have the Bottle Dungeon!' declared the castle guide, with a lugubrious relish. The dungeon, beyond its narrow mouth, swelled out twenty feet below us into an unimaginable prison. As the man said, it was indeed a bottle-shaped hellhole. 'You'll see,' the guide told us, 'that the floor of the dungeon is concave, so the prisoners could not lie down or stand up – but,' he added with a turn of the thumbscrew, 'their legs were probably broken anyway after they were thrown into the pit.'

We were entranced. 'Even worse than National Service,' Peter murmured. The ghoulish guide was into his stride now, detailing the torments of 'the martyr George Wishart – he was burrrned at the stake'. The rolling

Scots 'Rs' roared like a furnace around the unhappy Wishart one more time.

We reeled out into the grey afternoon, spluttering with suppressed giggles. The Bottle Dungeon and its ghastly keeper became a regular pilgrimage, as we returned time and again to sample the guide from hell and his unchanging recital of horrors. Time and again the prisoners were tossed into the pit, yet again the luckless George Wishart went up in flames. I struggle to understand why the thing had such a hold on us.

Weekends in Crail felt endless. A dismal sign on the local links said it all: 'No Sunday Golf'. The Music Box Café was closed, of course, and watching the fishing boats in Crail harbour was hardly an unmissable spectacle. The NAAFI club on camp – lukewarm tea, egg and chips, and ping pong – had a diminishing appeal. And naturally there was no television. Even the supply of Sunday papers delivered by the Corporal of the Horse, who had somehow secured the franchise, did little to fill the long hours. Along with other bored Linguists, I ventured on local trains as far as Perth and Dundee. As we rattled over the Tay Bridge, we chanted the ludicrous epic by Britain's best bad poet, William McGonagall, about a nineteenth-century railway disaster:

> Beautiful Railway Bridge of the Silv'ry Tay
> Alas I am very sorry to say
> That ninety lives have been taken away
> On the last sabbath day of 1879
> Which will be rememb'red for a very long time.

When we got to Dundee, we found it was shut as well.

Getting out of camp at weekends took on the frantically ingenious quality of an Escape from Colditz. For a while, there was a competition to see who could hitch-hike furthest and get back in time for parade on Monday morning. One intrepid escapee made it as far as John O'Groats, but then had to scuttle back by train.

Every few weeks I hoisted my kitbag and made my own break for freedom. Looking back now on those epic journeys home, armed with a forty-eight-hour weekend pass, I wonder what drove me to embark on the ordeal time and again. It meant a 500-mile round trip involving a nail-biting leapfrog between uncertain trains and rural buses – with a few hours at home before scampering back to the edge of Scotland.

Home by now was a neat semi on the outskirts of Halifax with a prospect of a green hillside, and a room of my own. My parents had moved out of the spooky flat over the record shop while I was in Crail, and I instantly loved my new haven. Tucked under the eaves, and furnished with a record player and a gas fire, it soothed away memories of my spartan bedroom overlooking Market Balcony. It seemed worth the trek from Crail for the brief joy of not waking up alongside thirty other young men in a hut.

There was also a new girlfriend back in Halifax, but that did not seem too promising. Maureen's mum and dad ran a pub, where she lived, and picking her up at home I immediately felt sucked into the close family embrace. Maureen's own embrace was more elusive. She was a keen churchgoer, and I expended precious week-end hours slumped beside her in an uncomfortable pew at St Jude's. It felt as interminable as those church parades during basic training. The prospect of a fumbled snog on the back row of the Odeon was a scant reward for my reluctant devotions or my heroic journey. Sometimes, she didn't even take off her gloves.

I suppose those crazed weekends were an updated version of dashing home from school for lunch, checking that there was still firm ground under the earthquake of my new life. But heading back to the station on a Sunday evening and the certainty of sitting up all night in a train packed with National Servicemen mooning about their girlfriends, I always decided this was the last time.

To this day, I am left behind by the cult of steam trains. As I tottered my kitbag down the platform at Edinburgh Waverley station, past the snorting beast which had hauled me up and over the border, the complacent smile of the driver wiping his greasy hands on a rag failed to stir me with notions of the heroic engineman. For me, the romance of steam remained unfathomable, particularly after rattling through the night in a smelly train, trying to pummel a few minutes of sleep from my kitbag pillow. I can still taste the memory of those unforgiving seats, marinated with the bitter railway stink of old smoke and unwashed passengers. Just occasionally, I got lucky and managed to scramble up into the improvised hammock of a luggage rack.

The end of my mad forty-eight hours involved a

panicky trot at first light over the fields outside Crail, trying to beat the 8 a.m. deadline for morning parade. A long day fighting to stay awake through the drizzle of new word lists was the final penalty for these brief encounters with the world beyond the JSSL stockade.

5

As the days lengthened in the spring of 1957, the morning parades were redeemed by the spectacle of the Isle of May glittering across the Firth of Forth in the crisp April sunshine. At JSSL, things were getting serious. Our Russian course turned increasingly from those cosy encounters with Pushkin poems to no-nonsense instruction in military matters. Now the word lists felt more like an arms dealer's catalogue. 'Bren-guns' did battle with 'howitzers', 'rolling barrages' menaced 'arms dumps'. I learned the Russian for 'athwartships', though nobody seemed to know what it meant in English.

Those teaching dialogues left behind the domestic soap operas of the early weeks with their cheery exchanges about shopping or entertaining friends – 'What a cosy room! What a good piano!' – 'The children are playing and I am repairing the fence.' Now, the little dramas were set 'In a Soviet People's Court' or 'In a Soviet Concentration Camp'. It was troubling enough to follow the fortunes of the 'Young Prisoner' who 'spent twelve months in the Lubianskaya Prison' and might expect 'only nine grams of bread a day – the weight of a Soviet Rifle bullet'. Even more alarming was the imagined ordeal of the 'British Sergeant', arrested after straying into Soviet territory and interrogated by an 'Investigating Officer of the MVD'. 'Why did you need a camera?' the fearsome MVD man asks. 'I wanted to take a few snapshots of my sweetheart,' offers the doomed Sergeant. 'Don't lie!' yells the MVD man. 'We know that you're a spy. We'll shoot you if you don't tell us the truth.'

Suddenly our weekly teaching booklets acquired pictures. A childlike drawing of a Soviet soldier stared out from the page, a socialist Action Man, every item of uniform listed in the margins. The next week, a double-page spread featured the badges of dozens of Soviet military units. I was particularly taken with that of the airforce transport unit, which appeared to be a back axle with wings. Then there was a drawing of a MiG fighter plane with the guts of the thing exposed like those anatomies of cruise liners or racing cars in boys' magazines.

Some of the dialogues began to feel uncomfortably close to home. 'I was assigned to a school of guerrilla activity. Much attention was devoted to foreign languages. We were flown behind enemy lines with radio equipment and boxes of weapons and ammunition.' I see that I have drawn a remarkably detailed skeleton in the margin of this scary little episode.

I wondered with a faint unease why I would ever need to know these things. The Cold War might have been making the world shiver, but very little of that reality or my possible involvement with it ever penetrated the walls of our classrooms. None of our teachers ever strayed into geopolitics, and in fact there seemed to be an embargo on politics of any kind. There was no attempt to indoctrinate us in our future role as fighters for the free world – the very idea would have made most of us laugh out loud. A JSSL tie was produced, a tasteful crest on a sober blue background, available for eleven shillings and ninepence – half a week's wages. There were few takers.

JSSL remained a world of its own, marooned at the end of a Scottish road to nowhere. In those years communications remained in many ways becalmed in the era of Jane Austen. A couple of Linguists reported being badgered by intrepid journalists who had slogged all the way to the camp gates on the fruitless hunt for a story about the secret spy school. I doubt whether tales of Russian irregular verbs would have thrilled the readers of the *News of the World*. Mostly, our isolation was complete. I don't recall making a single phone call over the months I was in Crail, and our only link to the outside world was by mail. Armed with our Waterman fountain pens and Basildon Bond notepaper, we wrote letters.

The daily distribution of post was a key beat in the rhythms of life. Small dramas of love and loss came with those letters from home. My letters from Maureen were mostly a recital of her comings and goings at the church youth club. I was beginning to wonder if she was a bit dim, but that might just have been malice driven by thwarted lust. Mostly, my comrades drifted away to read their letters behind a hut. Just occasionally, their faces as they scanned the latest news would give away a hint of those other lives, left behind with their civilian clothes but still tugging at them. In those years when real men didn't cry, most of this was kept bottled up. In the hothouse proximity of the dormitory, where we conducted most of our lives within two feet of the man in the next bedspace, there was little opportunity to bare our souls. Only a major tragedy like the death of someone in the family was permitted to break the surface – even triggering a few days of compassionate leave.

I wrote compulsively, to my parents, to the new girlfriend, to old school chums. God knows what I found to write about, given the unvarying routines of life at JSSL and the restrictions on writing openly about what we were doing. I doubt whether anyone would have been much interested anyway in hearing about my toils with Russian grammar. A day out at the St Andrews Bottle Dungeon or a trip to the Music Box Café filled out many a letter, starved of richer material.

I had another reason for writing all those letters. I needed to show off my new skill – italic handwriting. It must speak volumes for the limited access to entertainment in my life during those months that I chose to fill my spare moments with poring over a manual of calligraphy and re-inventing my personal alphabet. Maybe my nerdy immersion among so many swotty young men had something to do with it. Maybe I was remotely inspired by the monk Cyril's Russian alphabet. Maybe it was an attempt to carve out some kind of individuality amid the production line of JSSL. Whatever my motive, I spent long evenings in the reading room, struggling to refashion my scruffy schoolboy handwriting into the elegant shapes prescribed in the manual. I can still find my early efforts in the margins of a weekly study booklet. Alongside an explanation of 'parenthetical expressions' – 'Certainly a soldier must obey an officer' – I have laboriously penned fragments from a Gerard Manley Hopkins poem '. . . stirred for a bird' . . . 'gash gold vermilion'. For a moment, it seems that my schoolboy yearnings and naïvetés have spilled on to the page.

Out in the real world, where Victorian poetry and italic handwriting didn't feature in anyone's hit parade, it was a dangerous time. In May 1957, Britain successfully tested its first hydrogen bomb. The terrible blossoming of the thing in the South Pacific marked another escalation in the Armageddon stakes of the Cold War. I was coming to the end of my time out of that war at a moment when the prospects looked more bleak than ever.

In June 1957, the first anniversary of my National Service sentence, my fledgling life as a spy approached its moment of truth. All those mini ordeals of the weekly test would culminate in final exams to settle our fates for the rest of National Service. The hundreds of hours of immersion in the Russian language, the long march through the word lists, the months of grafting in the stifling little classrooms, would be judged in a few hours of tests.

We all knew the stakes. Those final exams at Crail had the brutal logic of one of the game shows which were starting to show up on the new commercial TV channel – *Take Your Pick* for a £1,000 prize or an old kipper. Our winners would get the top prize of spending the rest of their National Service at Cambridge University, leaving behind their uniforms and all things military. Our kipper candidates would be deemed to have failed the course and be dropped through a trapdoor back into the awful realities of National Service, being yelled at while cleaning latrines.

For those dutiful toilers who managed a respectable pass mark, the future meant life as a 'translator'. None of us had any real idea what this might mean, and nobody seemed inclined to tell us. There were dark hints of spooky assignments in shady places.

Finally, the results were posted in the usual place of torment – the noticeboard just inside the main gate. I jostled for a sight of the board, heart pounding, fearing the worst. I saw first that Peter had made it to Cambridge – of course. My name wasn't among the elect. But thank God I wasn't on the shorter list of those condemned to a life in the latrines. I had passed the Linguists' course.

All I knew about my future was that, along with my fellow survivors, I would be sent off to some place in Gloucestershire for yet more training. The intense time at the 'spy school' on the edge of Scotland came to an end in a confusion of kitbag stuffing and goodbyes. There was only a moment to say a hurried farewell to Peter with shared promises to stay in touch. Then we trundled down the long road out of camp and back to the world.

6

'FIFTEEN LOVE' ... '*Shassi vuipushkennii*' ... 'Da-da-da dum'. The tangled cacophony of Wimbledon commentaries and military Russian, all swamped by Beethoven's Fifth, bombarded me through the headphones. I struggled to extract something from the uproar and to scribble it down on my pad. At last, the torment came to a stop. The fierce-looking instructor seemed to have been schooled in a KGB interrogation centre. He looked over our logs without enthusiasm. '*Nye plocho – no nye dostatochno*,' he sneered. 'Not bad – but not good enough.'

Already, after just a few days at RAF Pucklechurch, my life as a spy was beginning to feel much more real. The camp was just up the hill from a pretty Gloucestershire village not far from Bristol. The village was as quaint as its name, a collection of stone cottages arranged round an ancient church, the kind of place that gets photographed for a jigsaw puzzle called 'Heart of England'.

My new RAF outpost was an altogether bleaker prospect. During World War II, the camp had been a barrage-balloon centre. Huge hangars had housed those silver whales I remember swimming in the skies of my wartime childhood, cuddly protectors against the evil German bombers. A decade after the war, the empty hangars still loomed over a scatter of wooden huts, casting a mournful shadow across the camp. This was to be my apprentice spy's finishing school.

With many of my fellow Linguists from Crail – the ones who hadn't been anointed to go to Cambridge – I was now to undergo what was called 'RAF orientation'. For eight weeks in the summer of 1957, we would be inducted into the peculiar freemasonry of our new trade. It was immediately obvious that Pushkin and Chekhov and those cosy domestic dialogues we'd come to know at Crail had no place here. The eccentric and unworldly teachers were also left behind, replaced now by a harder and more practical squad of commissars. In place of the romance of the Russian language, we were now to be force-fed military jargon and the stolid routines of Soviet aviation communications.

At last, the uncertainty over what JSSL was actually about began to resolve. From the first days at Pucklechurch, the elements of the next year of my life were laid out with clinical precision. The tools of my new trade as a cog in the Cold War sleuthing machine were basic enough. Learning to use them would be something else.

In the anonymous hut which was my new classroom, we got down to business immediately. Our weapons were issued: notepads, carbon paper, pencils and headphones. 'Your job will be to write down everything you hear,' barked the instructor with a head sleek as a badger. 'In order to maximize your efficiency, you will learn a shorthand which you must master. You must also attain complete fluency in numbers.' Without further introduction, he turned to a tape recorder as big as an oven. 'Put on your headphones. We will begin.'

For the next two months, it became the soundtrack of our lives. God knows who had the job of concocting this stew of Soviet pilots' chatter and miscellaneous interference. Symphonies and sports commentaries did battle with distorted intercom messages in an uproar which might have been devised by Stockhausen. Clearly, the idea was to prepare us for the challenges of trying to pluck Soviet communications from the ether. In fact, in the real world of monitoring, I don't recall ever encountering anything as messy and unfathomable as the noises blasted through our headphones in rural Gloucestershire.

We were drilled in the sparse shorthand required for recording the chatter of Soviet pilots and their controllers. It was hardly the stuff of a Cold War thriller. I began to wonder if the Soviets had contrived to replace their intrepid MiG pilots with robot speaking machines. 'I am climbing to' . . . 'My height is . . .' 'I am proceeding to . . .' 'I am descending to . . .' The controllers seemed even more tight-lipped. Their almost invariable response was '*Ponyal!*' – 'Understood.' When I eventually encountered the spartan exchanges of Beckett's and Pinter's characters, the repeating singsong of those Pucklechurch dialogues seemed to have found their laureates. The only relief was the accidental poetry of some of the technical codewords: '*Zelyonie goryat*' – literally 'Greens are burning' – seemed to hint at something more intriguing than the instructor's drab translation: 'My fuel warning lights are lit.'

Panning for these nuggets amid the murk of Wimbledon and Beethoven was a challenge made more wearying by its seeming pointlessness. As the weeks piled up, the headphones marked the passage of the hours in the monitoring classes with the red grooves on our ears. We were force-fed a diet of aircraft callsigns, which often seemed to have a surprisingly pastoral tone: 'Rain' and 'Acorn' and 'Willow'. We were bombarded with Russian numbers until they felt more familiar than their English equivalents. I had read somewhere about the 'brainwashing' of captured soldiers during the Korean War and I was coming to understand how it could work.

Just once, I realized it could have been worse. Between classes in the corridor of a teaching hut, I met up with a hollow-eyed Navy man. We traded stories and he told me he was training to be a Chinese Linguist. He hoped that by the end of his National Service, he might have some grasp of a basic alphabet.

OUR RADIO training at Pucklechurch was in the hands of Corporal Krasker, an splenetic little man with a talent for humiliation which would have equipped him well to be a drill instructor at some basic training hellhole. Struggling to try and tutor an endless supply of arty types and technical dunces who couldn't wire up a three-pin plug had clearly got to him. As I peered dismally into the dusty valves and wiring of a radio receiver, my repeated failure to identify what did what fuelled Krasker's limitless scorn. 'I've shat better objects than you,' he growled. I suspected at the time that Krasker's obsession with the insides of radios would hardly loom large in my life as a Russian Linguist. In fact I can't recall a single instance when my defective grasp of circuitry was ever an issue. For all of us, Krasker's technical torments ranked alongside the daily doses of PT we endured at Pucklechurch. Quite why our rulers felt it was useful preparation to pack our every spare moment with physical jerks in an old balloon hangar was just another mystery for bewildered Linguists who had long ago stopped looking for explanations.

Weekends in Pucklechurch yawned for ever. With Ivor and Stu, I explored the limited excitements of 50s Bristol, or sprawled on my bed in camp, reading, and writing letters. For weeks I had been looking forward to a visit from Maureen, who was planning a pony-trekking holiday in the Cotswolds. We had arranged to meet up on a Saturday afternoon during her trip, and in my frustrated imagination I had constructed a rural idyll, decorated with a tethered pony and a hidden copse. Then the day before we were due to meet, I got a letter from her telling me briskly that she would be too busy with the ponies to fit in a get-together. I tore up the letter and cursed the fickleness of women. I consoled myself that she couldn't spell either.

Escaping from Pucklechurch for the odd weekend at home was almost as daunting as the marathon of fleeing Crail. Once again, trekking across fields and leapfrogging between trains was the inevitable price of a few hours in a world without callsigns and numbers. Again, I usually wondered why I'd bothered. I trailed home late on Friday night, and slept until late morning on Saturday. I luxuriated in the latest crop of jazz records, shut away in my yellow bedroom with the caressing noises of Chet Baker and Stan Getz. I tootled hopelessly with a clarinet and produced animal squeaks. One Saturday morning a letter arrived from Maureen bidding me a polite farewell. There seemed to be a rival in the frame – equipped with the solid prospect of a family quarrying fortune. I hoped he enjoyed church.

Back on the market for a girlfriend, in the few hours left before I trudged back to the RAF, on Sunday afternoon I joined the Half Way House crowd. Since my schooldays, the little shop in the middle of the playing fields near St Jude's church had been a weekend magnet for teenagers – larking about, flirting, hanging around. Cigarettes were flaunted, lemonade was drunk. When I was in the sixth form, a bike with gears and drop handlebars, which thrust the cyclist's backside upwards like a chimp in heat, guaranteed the attention of the girls. I was all too aware that my 'sit-up-and-beg' model, like something from a country vicarage, complete with a basket, would not have done the trick. Now I found there was a new object of desire: the Lambretta. For some reason, these funny little motor scooters were suddenly sexy – probably because they featured in a couple of steamy Italian films where Gina Lollobrigida clung on to some hunk dashing through Rome on one of them. Now the new sex machine had arrived at the Half Way House, piloted, I noted bitterly, by a kid who had been a year below me at school but had managed to elude National Service by going straight to the new North Staffordshire Polytechnic. Even my bitchy reflection that it wasn't a real university wasn't much consolation. Another Lambretta spluttered to a halt, ridden by an even younger poser. This one was shamelessly red. It wasn't exactly Marlon Brando and his bikers in *The Wild One*, but the girls flocked around. It was time for me to start the trek back to Pucklechurch.

There was a joke in America at the time which targeted the soporific feel of the mid-1950s: 'Get the Eisenhower Doll – you wind it up and it does nothing for eight years.' The Hollywood films I occasionally caught on those fleeting Saturday nights at the Halifax Regal often celebrated the unruffled Pleasantville of Moms in their shining kitchens fixing dinner for Pops who would burst through the door with a cheery, 'Hi, honey, I'm home!' I went to see *The Pajama Game* and fell in love with the achingly pert Doris Day and her improbably pert bosom. In the street afterwards, 50s Yorkshire delivered its soggy smack of reality. Those American carryings-on were all very well, but standing in the rain at the bus stop on Commercial Street – that was the stuff of real life. Doris might have her wondrous pyjamas; our sensible Yorkshire version of 50s stagnation was made of lino and unheated bedrooms and sensible shoes.

Years into the new Elizabethan era, life in my northern town seemed to preserve many of the tight-lipped tendencies my mother often recounted from her own girlhood before World War I. Curtains still twitched at any suggestion of 'gallivanting'. The hottest night available was the Saturday night dance in a school assembly hall, twirling stiffly against the voluminous underskirts of a gawky partner to the accompaniment of a three-piece band – balding men on accordion, alto sax and drums. If you got really lucky you might manage a last waltz, and a brief snog on the way to the bus. Getting your girlfriend 'in the family way' was a disaster which could be tidied away only by a speedy trip to the altar. Condoms were rumoured to be available at the alarming shop where they displayed trusses and surgical boots; but who would dare to go through the door and face the matron in the white coat? Bosses and teachers and doctors wielded unquestioned authority. The death penalty was still in full swing. I had never met anyone whose parents had been divorced. A cousin, who had already joined his father as a jobbing builder, greeted every challenge life threw at him – from falling off a ladder to dislocating his wrist while playing cricket – with the same stoical slogan: 'You have it to do.'

But though it was often hard to detect, especially from inside the fence of an RAF gulag, there was a feeling in the air that at last, a dozen years after the end of World War II, things in Britain might be looking up. A new prime minister was telling us that we'd 'never had it so good', and even in the depths of my National Service incarceration there were hints of change.

The trusty BBC was being abruptly shouldered aside by the noisy and insistent commercial upstarts on button three. *Double Your Money*, with its audience baying for instant cash, kicked sand in the face of the venerable *Animal, Vegetable, Mineral?*, with its professors pondering the provenance of an Etruscan nose flute. Commercial TV news stripped its newsreaders of those BBC dinner jackets, and there were even regional accents to be heard.

In February 1957 the 'Toddlers' Truce' came to an end. Until then, in a self-denial unimaginable by kids raised under today's torrential television barrage, the Truce had kept TV screens dark from 6 p.m. to 7 p.m. every evening so that toddlers could spend time with parents before being put to bed. Now, all that was blown away by the *Six-Five Special*. British television's first pop programme was introduced by Pete Murray with an excruciating attempt at hip talk: 'We've got almost a hundred cats jumping here, some real cool characters to give us the gas.' Britain's emergent teenagers were galvanized.

My parents' music shop was suddenly invaded by the raucous noise of rock 'n' roll. In fact the shop even played a tiny part in the rock 'n' roll assault on Britain. For months, a beefy Halifax trombonist called Gordon Langhorn had tested my father's boundless tolerance by hanging around for hours at a time sampling new instruments. Suddenly, reborn as 'Don Lang and His Frantic Five', he became a Star of *Six-Five Special*. My father was delighted to see big Gordon head off to his destiny in London.

Tommy Steele and Adam Faith and Cliff Richard, our home-grown Elvises, threatened to shout down the cosy British ballads of Ruby Murray and David

Whitfield. From the snotty heights of my modern jazz passions, I prowled around the shop on those Saturday afternoon escapes from Russian, hating it all. But even I had to admit that anything was better than Whitfield's mawkish hit 'The Book' – a classic of the pre-rock fifties, extolling the virtues of a family bible. After that, even Tommy Steele's awful 'Rock with the Caveman' felt like a breath of fresh air.

Back in Pucklechurch opportunities for sedition were thin on the ground, but Eddie and his chums managed to pull off a stunt which blew a raspberry at several cherished institutions. Eddie was a good mimic, and with his friends he organized a mock royal broadcast to be relayed on the camp's public address system. Catching to perfection the tones of the young Queen Elizabeth, he recorded a state opening of the camp ablutions, complete with massed flushing toilets. Our RAF rulers were of course aghast at this unthinkable act of treason, which contrived to combine seizure of military property with ridicule of the monarch. There was a big fuss, but we were coming to the end of our course. After the long investment in our training, even the shocking display of lèse-majesté could not be allowed to delay the dispatch of a single recruit for the front line of the Cold War. As Corporal Krasker memorably put it: 'You're having an exam next week, and by the way you've all passed.'

Half-way through my National Service sentence, it was time for the nation to recoup its investment in my sleuthing. Ten months after my first encounter with the Russian alphabet, I was about to find out what it was all for.

LESLIE WOODHEAD

It was still unclear what might happen next, but some outlines were emerging from the mists of military evasion. It seemed some of us would be posted to mysterious outposts in Britain. The rest would be shipped off to some fault line of the Cold War – wherever that might be. A few bold spirits declared a taste for adventure, swapping Biggles fantasies about being parachuted into Siberia. Most of us were inclined to hope for an inconspicuous Nissen hut somewhere in the home counties.

The Signals Intelligence batallions I was about to join had originally been founded soon after World War II as a kind of crude early warning system. A handful of Russian speakers listened out through headphones to hear if the Soviet bombers were coming. By the early 1950s there were fears that the Russians were winning the intelligence war. The British super-spies Burgess and Maclean had plundered Western secrets; high-tech Soviet bugging devices had been found in Western embassies around the world. The successes of brainwashing in Korea triggered alarms of Communist thought control. For years, Allied intelligence efforts concentrated on parachuting agents into Russia, or dropping them off from fast patrol boats in the Baltic. By the mid-50s, Western Intelligence concluded that all the agents had been captured and made to transmit false information. It was obvious that agent operations were a disaster. The focus of Allied espionage turned to electronic eavesdropping and signals monitoring – which was to be where the Russian Linguists joined the story.

All of this was of course concealed behind layers of

official bureaucracy and secrecy. But approaching the end of my training, it was time for me to join the conspiracy. As we waited to hear our fates, we were required to complete one final ritual before being admitted to the freemasonry of spooks. With my fellow Linguists, all now branded on our sleeves with the single inverted stripe of our new promotions to the rank of RAF Junior Technician (four pounds, seven shillings and sixpence per week), I was marched to a hut on the edge of camp. A sombre-looking officer was waiting for us. It was clear that this was more than yet another routine pep talk.

'Now pay attention,' he began. 'Today we have a very serious business. You will all be required now to sign the Official Secrets Act. This is a solemn undertaking, with solemn obligations.' Displaying some relish, he proceeded to spell out those hair-raising obligations. 'Under Section One of the Act, if you disclose information useful to an enemy, or prejudicial to the safety interests of the State, you may be imprisoned for fourteen years.' But that, he would have us understand, wasn't all. 'Under Section Two, if you pass on any information, however insignificant, about your Linguists' training or about the Royal Air Force, you could face two years in prison.'

My mind raced like a hamster in a wheel to recall what I might have let slip to friends or family. Had I told anyone about the brand of carbon paper we used, or the grade of pencil? In the stunned silence, it was obvious that my comrades were chasing round their own hamster wheels. No one spoke as we queued up to sign the fearsome Act. Finally, there was no escaping the realization that this was for real. It felt as if a draught from the Cold War had whistled under the door.

We were lined up and injected like a herd of cattle. All that was left was to hear where we were going to be posted. The bleak official shorthand was that we would be proceeding to our 'user units'. That early autumn of 1957 was a time of gathering international paranoia. The Soviets launched Sputnik, and as the world's first satellite beeped its way round the planet, everything and everywhere suddenly seemed vulnerable. America and Russia brandished their new intercontinental ballistic missiles at one another, and we learned about a new nightmare called 'the four-minute warning'. The cinemas were flooded with apocalyptic sci-fi shockers like *The Night the World Exploded!* and *The Monster That Challenged the World!* ('Crawling up from the depths . . . to terrify and torture!')

So what were the Russkis up to? What fiendish schemes were they concocting behind the walls of the Kremlin? Was the Soviet army about to invade the Vienna Opera House? Were those MiGs with the scary red stars heading to strafe Lord's cricket ground? It was into this toxic atmosphere of fear and suspicion that my career as a mini-spy was about to be launched. It was still hard to believe that our efforts with pencils and carbon paper could make a difference; but it was clear at last that we might have some kind of purpose as footsoldiers in the Cold War.

At the end of September 1957, I found myself jostling with an anxious crowd of freshly qualified Linguists for a glimpse of one more noticeboard which would define the next chapter of my life. I pushed my way to the front and found my name. I was on the list headed BERLIN.

7

I HOPED I wasn't going to be sick. Battened down
below decks with hundreds of other National Servicemen being shipped off to Germany, I muttered a snatch
of some half-remembered poem Rupert Brooke had
written on his way across the Channel to the trenches:
'The damn ship lurched and slithered . . .' The soldier
on the opposite bunk looked decidedly green. I tried to
hold on to the thought that the voyage from Harwich
to the Hook of Holland couldn't last much longer. The
old troopship rolled again, like a wallowing sow.

I had crossed the Channel a couple of times before,
on school trips heading for Switzerland. Then there had
been the shared excitements of running round the deck,
the thrill of escape from home, an overnight adventure
on a train reeking of Gauloises. Cramped up now on a
metal bunk in the belly of the boat, surrounded by rows
of other bunks and other servicemen, I felt like helpless
cargo in a cattle transporter.

Still, even in the bowels of that National Service
ferry, I discovered in myself a flicker of expectation. I
was heading for somewhere edgy and different, an exotic

place on the front line of the Cold War. This wouldn't be like anything I had ever known on those brief school trips to postcard-pretty Swiss villages, rambling through alpine meadows where the most threatening prospect was a bad-tempered cow.

In those years before the big jets shrunk the planet, blurring the oddness and difference of other places, Berlin haunted the imagined landscape of my generation. All my childhood, it had stood for a heart of darkness, a source of terrible things. Berlin was where that bomber had come from, the one I saw trapped in a searchlight as my mother hurried me to the air-raid shelter in Glasgow. Berlin was the place in those photos my father had brought back from a band trip to Germany in the thirties, the pictures with swastikas hanging from the buildings, the ones that stayed shut away in a drawer. Somehow, even aged eight, I knew Berlin was the reason behind those terrible newsreels just after the war which had made a man throw up near me in the cinema. My head swam as I tried to untangle those piles of impossibly spindly bodies, bulldozed into pits, limbs flopping.

I had also seen the newsreels of a ruined Berlin, the camera brooding over a wilderness of devastation where nothing moved. More recently, Berlin had become the victim. The newsreels had shown a city threatened with strangulation. Marooned inside Communist East Germany since World War II had left Hitler's capital in ruins, in 1948 Berlin had been throttled by Stalin after he cut off all supply routes into the city. Then the newsreels in the Halifax Odeon had rallied behind the

Berlin airlift and the desperate Allied effort to fly in relief supplies. A triumphal soundtrack accompanied the flood of aircraft deluging Berlin, and the welcoming crowds of ragged people. I remembered children scuffling for sweets thrown from a cockpit window.

Now I had a special reason for recalling the airlift. A main artery for that vital transfusion of supplies had been RAF Gatow. And RAF Gatow was the destination on the Movement Order in my pocket, the base where I would do my bit as a footsoldier in the intelligence war.

Clambering into the train on the dockside in Holland for the long slog into Germany, I suddenly felt I was leaving behind more than training camps and home. As I hoisted my kitbag into the compartment on a serious brown German train, I experienced a naïve teenage epiphany – self-dramatizing, I suppose, but it felt, at that moment, genuine. This could be where adult life began, I thought, heading into unknown territory on important business. Looking across the compartment at the Linguists who had been with me since Crail, I saw the familiar teenage faces – Ivor and Ron and Stu and Ray – and just felt glad not to be heading into that unknown territory on my own.

Although I had only a sketchy understanding of what awaited me in this place which seemed overloaded with awful history, I had picked up a few scraps about the schizophrenic state of Berlin twelve years after the war. I gathered the devastated city had been carved up between the four Great Powers, and was now divided into sectors which mimicked the Cold War standoff.

The ultimate barrier of the Berlin Wall was still years in the future, but the city was already a mad mosaic of power and suspicion. The three Western heavyweights, Britain, America and France, patrolled their bits of Berlin, watching out for the fretful Soviet behemoth just down the street. The newsreels had told me that this uncertain stalemate was being played out 100 miles inside Communist territory, but I couldn't imagine what that might mean.

All day we rolled through West Germany, Essen and Dortmund, places dimly remembered from the war, gorging in the dining-car, feeling more like tourists than brand-new spies. It was dark when we arrived in Hanover, on the edge of Communist Europe. We were shunted off into the NAAFI club on the station, and stuffed with yet more food. Just before midnight, in a scene borrowed from some *film noir*, complete with searchlights stabbing through steam and sinister-looking guards, we were bundled on to the train for Berlin.

A military policeman barged into our compartment and yanked down the window blind. 'Soviet regulations,' he said, 'while we're passing through the Zone.' From what I'd glimpsed of the featureless gloom of Communist East Germany, it seemed a bit over the top. I fell asleep, and came awake to find an East German border guard, complete with Kalashnikov, demanding my papers. I had an instant stab of alarm – maybe he'll know what I'm doing here, and haul me off somewhere. After a curt glance, he was gone, and the train clattered on again.

If I had been aware of something then that I only

heard about more than forty years later, I might have been even more jumpy. It seems that those nightly troop trains through Communist territory sometimes carried an unannounced passenger. Crouched in a lavatory with the 'Engaged' sign on the door, a sleuth with a radio receiver would spend the night trying to eavesdrop on Soviet communications. I suspect the soldier with the Kalashnikov might have paid our compartment another visit if he'd ferreted out the spook in the loo.

On a sunny autumn morning, our train rumbled into the Zoo station in West Berlin. Our little squad of newly minted eavesdroppers was herded on to buses and ferried through streets which only a dozen years ago had been piles of rubble. At first sight the city looked surprisingly prosperous as we passed along wide avenues fringed by new blocks of flats. There seemed to be well-stocked shops and pavement cafés. There was no hint of the blitzed city I had read about, plagued by epidemics and starvation. Soon we were in the western suburbs, crossing a bridge and a river. A sign for the Olympic Stadium stirred a chilling memory of Hitler's 1936 celebration of Nazi might and order. The bus turned into a quiet leafy road, with glimpses of a lake between comfortable-looking houses and bungalows. Then suddenly, we were there – a neat pebble-dashed gatehouse, 'Royal Air Force Gatow' over the entrance.

Bleary after our two-day journey, we peered out of the window at our new home. An avenue of trees lined the immaculate road, a mosaic of cobbles as perfect as a snake's skin, leading into the heart of the base. It all looked resolutely tidy, with a Teutonic orderliness which almost made me yearn for the shabby wooden huts and sagging barbed wire of Crail or Pucklechurch. We stopped outside a substantial two-storey building. 'This is it' said the escorting officer. As I slugged my kitbag out of the bus, I looked up and noticed a sculpted head staring out from over the doorway. It seemed to be a pilot in a leather flying-helmet and goggles. The officer noticed my curiosity. 'He's a Nazi flying ace,' he said, 'one of Goering's finest. If you haven't been told, this used to be the Luftwaffe's training headquarters, designed by Hitler's architect Albert Speer.'

Goering certainly knew how to treat his boys, I thought, as we tramped upstairs. On a corridor as spotless as a sanatorium, we were allotted our rooms. I threw my kitbag on to a bed and surveyed my living space for the next nine months. After the spartan drabness of the billets I'd known, this looked like luxury. A mellow wood-block floor replaced the inevitable brown lino, a chunky central-heating radiator banished memories of filthy coke stoves, snug double glazing mocked the draughty windows of Crail and Pucklechurch. Best of all, instead of living like a gerbil piled up alongside thirty other gerbils, just three of us would share this cosy nest.

I had got lucky. My room-mates were both congenial chaps I had known since Crail. There was Dick Simms, a lanky salt-of-the-earth type from rural Northamptonshire, who had displayed patience beyond the ordinary under sustained joshing about his roots in Thrapston 'amid the mangel-wurzels'. And there was Ron Akehurst, a sardonic Londoner with Buddy Holly glasses and a shambling appearance which felt like a calculated snub of all things military. As we dragged crumpled items from our kitbags, unsettled by the vision of German prosperity, we shared curmudgeonly mumblings along the lines of 'Who won the bloody war anyway?'

Amid the mess of unpacking, I slumped at the table under the window and wrote a note to my parents. I felt the need to check in from this place a long way from home. Even the address the RAF had given us felt like a kind of cover:

5024056 J/T Woodhead LJ,
Signals Section,
Royal Air Force,
Gatow,
Berlin, BFPO 45

– my place in the new scheme of things.

In the afternoon we were assembled for a pep talk from a Wing-Commander. It felt more like a warning. We were reminded that Berlin was an island surrounded by an ocean teeming with Communist sharks. The perimeter fence of RAF Gatow itself was also the boundary of the Soviet Zone. 'Sometimes, we can see tanks,' he said. There was more along these lines. 'As Linguists, you're barred from travelling on the S-Bahn – that's the overhead railway. It runs into East Germany, so if you fall asleep you could find yourself having an uncomfortable time with the Stasi – they're the East German Secret Police, and they're not nice to people they think are spies. That actually happened to a couple of your predecessors, so be warned.' Finally, the Wing-

Commander had a more personal warning. 'Watch out for the girls touting for business outside the NAAFI club on Reichskanzlerplatz. You could catch something nasty.'

The next morning, we went to work.

8

BERLIN IN THE Cold War was a spy's paradise. The city was the control centre of the Soviet Empire in Eastern Europe. But Berlin's location also made it a perfect Trojan horse in the heart of the enemy citadel. Marooned after World War II inside Communist East Germany, it provided a platform from which the West could snoop on the Commies and plunder secrets at will. In the 1950s, Berlin was the base for the largest British Secret Intelligence operation in the world. A hundred spooks maintained swarms of support staff; special units tracked down information about Soviet and East German forces; others sniffed around for political and scientific intelligence. A gang of snoopers laboured to penetrate Soviet headquarters in East Berlin.

Spying was also a welcome contributor to the local economy. British agent and Soviet superspy George Blake reported that after the decline of the Berlin black market in the early 50s, many Berliners were working as part-time intelligence gatherers for both sides. Energetic locals even managed to hold down several sleuthing jobs at the same time.

Some of the more resourceful sons and daughters of Socialism became part of 'Operation Tamarisk', one of the murkier activities of the espionage war. This involved scuffling through Communist waste-paper baskets and garbage bins to dig out promising scraps. The unlovely harvest was then shipped to the West where it was sifted by unenviable analysts – some of them, I came to know, JSSL graduates

That was not the worst assignment which might land in the lap of a JSSL man. Some of their most prized material was actually gleaned from Soviet toilet paper. The Red Army's reluctance to squander resources on decadent capitalist loo rolls meant that troops on exercise in East Germany had to improvise. So Private Ivan and Corporal Igor had to wipe their bottoms on scraps of code books and maps. As a result, the shit-stained cast-offs of the People's Army became a rich source of intelligence for dedicated toilers back in the free world. JSSL men based in Whitehall found themselves with the unlovely job of translating toilet paper. Their efforts as part of 'Operation Tamarisk' were considered one of the most successful intelligence gathering initiatives over the fifty years of the Cold War.

Before I arrived to join the fun, a Cold War spectacular known as the Berlin Tunnel had been gushing Communist secrets into the troughs of western intelligence for years. The story of the tunnel is a perfect fable of the determination, ingenuity and lunacy of Berlin espionage in the 1950s.

The tunnel project was a bizarre joint venture between the British Post Office, the US Air Force and the CIA. It sounds like an Ealing comedy, but it was in reality a top secret operation to tap into Soviet communications throughout the Communist world. In the 50s, telephone and telegraph links between Moscow, Warsaw and Bucharest all went via Berlin. Tipped off about the prospects by an agent in the East Berlin telephone exchange, for a year from February 1954 the Allies excavated the tunnel under the Soviet sector of the city. Plugging into the Soviet underground cables, the operation churned out 40,000 hours of taped phone conversations, and 6 million hours of teletype messages as the nervous Allies trawled for hints that the Cold War might be about to boil. In those years before spy satellites, the torrent of information about Soviet orders of battle and troop dispositions was espionage treasure.

Though the Allies did not realize it, the Soviets, alerted by their agent George Blake, had spotted the tunnel more than a year before I arrived in Berlin and had been feeding dud material into the system. But in the crazed hall of mirrors that was Cold War spying, the Communist leadership in Moscow decided it was more important to protect Blake than to reveal their knowledge of the tunnel. In the spring of 1956, they developed a scheme to discover the tunnel 'accidentally' so as not to put Blake at risk. Inevitably, in the hothouse of Berlin sleuthing and counter-sleuthing, the Soviet digging operation to uncover the tunnel was spotted, and the Allies had evacuated long before the triumphant comrades arrived in a glare of prearranged publicity. As it happened, the tunnel operation had been finally shut down the day before I reached Berlin.

The British Military Exchange Mission had been established after World War II with the stated aim of fostering good working relations between the Allied and Soviet military occupiers in the divided Germany. The Brixmis logo declares its noble purpose with entwined Union Jack and Soviet flags. Behind the facade of shared monitoring, the outfit was credited with pulling off some of the most audacious and successful intelligence-gathering operations of the Cold War.

Under a Four Power Agreement which might have been drafted by Lewis Carroll, Allied and Soviet military inspectors from Brixmis and Soxmis were permitted to twitch the Iron Curtain and gain access to each other's military activities. As the only British military unit operating inside Communist East Germany, Brixmis was never officially a part of British Intelligence. But by stretching the limits of its liaison activities, from the 50s to the 80s, the outfit got away with plundering enemy secrets in a raffish style which would have gladdened the heart of Biggles.

The operations, carried out by observers in old saloon cars, were often pursued with devil-may-care boldness. Finding 'Mission Restricted' signs posted by the Cold War enemy, the patrols would regularly throw them in a ditch and press on. Several Brixmis veterans still cherish their 'Mission Restricted' ties, specially made by Gieves & Hawkes of Savile Row. More sober bystanders in British Military HQ and the Foreign Office were often alarmed. The KGB and the Stasi were equally unimpressed. Brixmis patrols were ambushed, rammed, beaten and shot at. Using a couple of Chipmunk training planes, Brixmis pilots snooped photos of military targets, sometimes dropping in to RAF Gatow to patch up bullet-holes acquired in the process.

It was Brixmis of course which got its hands dirty with Operation Tamarisk, the ghastly trawl through the detritus and even the bowels of the Cold War enemy. Brixmis veterans had a less evasive name for Tamarisk, dubbing it 'shit-digging'. Whatever the label, those unsavoury gleanings were still a prime source of intelligence thirty years later during the Soviet occupation of Afghanistan.

Even now, it all sounds both improbable and immensely risky. And of course Soxmis, the Soviet counterpart of Brixmis, was carrying out its own sleuthing raids on Allied military operations, visiting places closed to official diplomats, running agents and supporting them. Why on earth did both sides feel it was worth carrying out these wild escapades at the very limits of provoking World War III? The continuation of this dangerous dance over four decades was a nonstop sideshow of the Cold War carnival. A memorable film of the period, *The Defiant Ones*, told the story of a couple of escaped convicts, one black and one white, chained together on the run, painfully learning that their survival depended on their cooperation. It was like a metaphor for the mutual embrace of the superpowers. Somewhere in the exhausting business of preserving this eternal stalemate, I was now to play my temporary part.

I was of course ignorant of these global melodramas as I marched out to begin my first spell of duty as a very junior spook. The morning after we arrived at RAF

Gatow, our little squad of raw newcomers was steered towards an anonymous building, inconspicuous behind pine trees on the edge of the base. As we got closer, it was impossible to miss the thicket of aerials bristling from the roof. This was the monitoring centre, the place which was about to become the focus of my life.

I heard that the Signals Detachment at Gatow had been born by chance. The story was that after the war, a German child had been playing with a VHF receiver dumped by the Americans and had suddenly tuned in on Soviet air communications. That sounded like a myth, I thought. I was now going to join the real story.

Military police, metal gates, security checks – all the paraphernalia of paranoia was on display to greet us. We were processed through a 'security cage', and led up a flight of stairs into a long darkened room, windows blanked out. At a series of benches, youths much like us crouched in front of glowing radio receivers tuned to various frequencies, headphones clamped to heads, pencils scribbling on pads. A sergeant surveyed the room from a platform, like a Victorian headmaster. The stink of old cigarettes and long nights hit us.

This is just as it should be, I thought, a spy centre which could have been created for a film. I could imagine Kenneth More or Jack Hawkins in cool command, fighting the good fight on behalf of the free world. The reality was the weary-looking sergeant and his rumpled group of eavesdroppers. They seemed very pleased to see us. I soon found out that it wasn't just a comradely welcome.

The overnight watch heaved themselves out of their

chairs, and the sergeant shuffled us into their places. 'Good luck,' my predecessor said, clamping his headphones over my ears as I slid into his seat. I felt like a relay runner grabbing the baton from a team mate without breaking stride. Clearly no fragment was allowed to get lost in the crack between shifts. 'It's pretty quiet on the frequency for now,' my forerunner advised. 'just "Dozhd Tridsats Shest" doing circuits and bumps.' Good old "Dozhd",' I thought, relieved to find that at least one of the callsigns we'd struggled to extract from the mess of music and mayhem at Pucklechurch had turned up in the real world. 'Dozhd', the Russian for 'rain', was obviously the John Smith of the MiG squadrons. It was reassuring to find him or at least his real life clone – far from Gloucestershire, somewhere in the murky skies of East Germany. The night watch reeled away to their beds, leaving us to face the Red Peril.

So this was it. I was actually on the front line, doing the job. As the static hissed in my headphones, I waited, pencil poised to report my first nugget of intelligence. Nothing disturbed the white noise filling my ears, no vital revelation of imminent invasion. Even faithful old Dozhd seemed to have nodded off. I looked around the gloomy room. Most of my colleagues seemed to be scribbling away, dutiful worker bees harvesting their intelligence pollen. I wondered if I dared to spin the dial and try to find some jazz on the American Forces Network, but the sergeant looked alert to any hint of deserting the frequency. The hissing in my ears was making me drowsy.

Suddenly, a harsh voice exploded in my earphones. I was engulfed in a torrent of Russian chatter, rapid exchanges between pilots and ground controllers. My pencil raced over the pad, my carbons fluttered, but I was swamped. I was only getting fragments of the stuff on paper. Gradually, I began to get the sense of what was going on. It was nothing more than a few pilots reporting in on weather in their area, and receiving forecasts. Realizing that I wasn't missing the start of World War III, I tried to winnow out the vital callsigns from the routine chatter. Then, as suddenly as it had begun, the storm of activity passed. I settled into logging scattered exchanges about course and altitude, requests for landing, reports on fuel levels.

I looked at my watch. Only seven hours and twenty minutes to the end of the shift. Only 6,048 hours to the end of National Service.

9

'*Dear Mum and Dad,*

I often wish that I could emulate the squirrels, finding a comfortable hollow tree to curl up and hibernate away the rest of my National Service, only waking every now and then on warm days for a nut or two. But doubtless the RAF would have something to say about that.'

A grey Sunday morning, a month into my new life as a worker ant in the Berlin spy heap. As I write, the remorselessly cheery programme *Two-Way Family Favourites* chatters from a radio somewhere. It has to be the soundtrack of National Service: record requests and dedications from parents and girlfriends for chaps in uniform, holed up in last-ditch British outposts round the world – Aden, Cyprus, Hong Kong, Malaya, Germany. 'It won't be long now, dear' messages are swapped by affable uncle Cliff Michelmore and mumsy Jean Metcalfe. I read somewhere that Jean's railway clerk father used to sponge his celluloid collar every night. Cliff and Jean were a famously married couple, and the spirit of wartime Vera Lynn lived on in the programme, that special British cordial of controlled yearning and chins-up fortitude.

The programme had also been the soundtrack of my Sunday lunchtimes at home in Halifax as my father toiled over the routines of re-ordering records sold out in the Saturday rush. The unvarying intro had been an inescapable part of those teenage Sunday mornings: 'The time in Britain is twelve noon. In Germany it's one o'clock. But home and away, it's time for *Two-Way Family Favourites*.' Then there came the saccharine signature tune, 'With a Song in My Heart'. In some way I couldn't have identified, *Two-Way Family Favourites* had congealed in my head in those years as the numbing centre of domestic tedium. Now I was on the receiving end of that familiar brew of much-loved British melodies and acceptable 50s pop: dashing Irish tenor Josef Locke warbling 'Hear My Song'; Richard Tauber belting out 'You Are My Heart's Delight'; Mantovani's strings swooning over 'Charmaine'. Just occasionally these days, Elvis butted in.

Now, on this Berlin Sunday morning, as the dutiful son pushed his fountain pen over the Basildon Bond, here came bloody Mantovani again.

Announced as 'British Forces Mail' in my effortful new italic handwriting, my letters recorded the mundane doings of my new life. 'Went into Berlin to change library books at the British Centre, but it was closed' . . . 'During my Berlin wanderings on Wednesday I found a newly opened record shop with an almost all-jazz bias' . . . 'We had some snow in the wind around Friday dinner time, but it didn't come to anything' . . .

In my last leave before heading to Berlin, during yet another youth club dance, I had managed to acquire a new girlfriend. She had just had a part in a play about Noah's Ark performed by local amateurs. She said she had played Ham's wife. Casting around for common ground in our early chat-up, we had talked about Shakespeare. Freed from the limitations of the departed Maureen, I tried to lure the new girfriend with news of my cultural activities: 'We're reading a couple of Shaws for our play reading group, so that should fill the weekend quite pleasantly' . . .

My 'Berlin wanderings' were timid adventures during those first weeks. Going into the city meant taking a bus and then a tram, braving the non-too-friendly glares of the local Berliners. We were not allowed to wear uniform off the base, but that did not seem to conceal our identity as members of the occupying forces. My Cambridge blazer badge, purchased as some kind of protector to see me through the National Service tunnel, didn't exactly help me to blend in. Even twelve years after the end of the war, there was no mistaking the hostility of some fellow passengers on those trips into town.

A fellow Linguist reported that he had had worrying personal experience of that hostility after an outing to a bar in Kladow, close to the Soviet section of the city. Heading for the bus, he and his friends had been threatened with a beating by a gang of German teenagers. 'We were only saved by the pleas of a girl we'd been drinking with,' he said.

For one uncertain teenager, dipping a toe into a foreign city for the first time was an unsettling business. Getting off the tram on one of my first ventures out, I watched a policeman chase 100 yards in pursuit of an unfortunate who had disobeyed the signs for crossing the road. Berlin seemed – well – very German.

I realized that my sense of the place which was my new home was somehow infused with the images of a film I had seen half a dozen years before. Heading out on a wet winter night, I had gone to the Electric Cinema in Halifax to see *The Third Man*. Unusually, I recall, my mother was with me. The dark brew of brooding photography, Viennese sewers, and the maddeningly addictive zither music stuck with me. Vienna was a different city in a different country, of course, but the film was set in a place which was also under Four Power occupation, like my Berlin built on layers of secrecy, deceit and betrayal. For me now, Graham Greene's powerfully imagined vision of a corrupted city and Carol Reed's claustrophobic film leaked on to the sunny streets of the new Berlin.

The reality seemed determined to cancel out those sinister expectations. My territory on those early explorations was usually limited to a trudge round the same beat. Like a nervous cub patrolling safe tracks, I kept close to the smart shops along the Kurfürstendamm in the city centre. The shiny treasures in their glass cases, jewellery and handbags and shoes, seemed like loot from a recent battle. I remembered the drab shop windows in Halifax with their frumpy dresses and sensible shoes, and wondered again who had really won the war. But looming at the end of the 'Ku-damm', as I knowingly called it after a couple of trips, was a shattered relic of Berlin's recent devastation. The Kaiser Wilhelm Memorial Church, with its steeple snapped off like a rotten stump, had become the symbolic centre of West Berlin. Just before I arrived in the city, the ruin had been the rallying point for an angry campaign by Berliners to preserve some memory of their pre-war buildings. With so many bombed landmarks heedlessly bulldozed aside in the rush to rebuild, much of the city's former character had been obliterated under a remorseless tide of concrete boxes.

The NAAFI club, the other safe haven in my early Berlin wanderings, certainly qualified as one of those concrete boxes. A dreary cube near my tram stop, it had the charm of a Soviet cement factory. But for a frozen and footsore serviceman a long way from home, it felt like nirvana. Keeping a lookout for those risky fräuleins the Wing-Commander had warned us about, I fell into the cosy British embrace of the club. The plywood and Formica tables were pure Halifax, the twenty-five-watt light bulbs brought back Market Balcony, the tepid cups of grey tea were just like Mother used to make. Even the murky little TV set in the corner offered memories of home.

But on my first visit to the NAAFI club, the TV was showing something completely unfamiliar. I stood in front of the set, transfixed by a picture of a thing like a football with an aerial sticking out of it. The thing was beeping. An excited boffin with wild hair informed us that this was Sputnik, the first satellite in space – and it was a Soviet satellite. My boyhood passion for the romance of astronomy and fantasy spaceships had always been fuelled by fanciful paintings of Saturn's rings and lurid sci-fi paperbacks with titles like *The Avenging*

Martian. Sputnik was suddenly and alarmingly real. Somehow, I felt involved with this new lurch in the Cold War. I had an instant cartoon-strip vision – I was listening in on them; but now they could look down on me, and on everyone else. I headed for the tram and RAF Gatow. My new home seemed even more exposed now.

It was a peculiarly schizophrenic aspect of life on the base that the rest of the inmates – clerks, cooks, military police, airmen getting on with their usual flightless tasks – were not supposed to have any idea of what we Linguists were up to in the monitoring building. On one occasion, even the Gatow base commander, a blustering RAF officer, was denied entry when he turned up unannounced at the security gate. It was only after several apoplectic minutes that he was grudgingly permitted to come inside and make an inspection of the scribbling monitors. I doubt whether he could make much of it. He resolved to get his own back by flying his Chipmunk over the base and sending messages on our monitoring frequencies. Told to get lost, his breezy reply was logged by one of my chums: 'Get off, you buggers! I'm flying up here.'

The mystery of what was going on out there on the edge of the base inevitably generated regular speculation in the canteen queues. There were envious hints along the lines of 'You smart arses are on a skive.' Of course I'm sure everybody had a pretty clear idea of what we were doing, disappearing every day into that strange building festooned with aerials. But for the most part, we remained insulated from the routines of RAF Gatow, and from the rest of its population.

Just occasionally, the mysterious Linguists collided with that other Gatow. One night after the three of us in our room had escaped into slumber, we were jolted awake by an uproar in the corridor. The door crashed open and the lights snapped on. Three privates from the fearsome Scottish Army regiment based at Gatow, which was known universally as 'the poison dwarfs', swayed in the doorway. They were clearly very drunk and very cross. Through the haze of their slurry Glaswegian and our drowsiness, we gathered they were hunting for an RAF policeman. We must have convinced them they were off-target. 'OK, then, dinna worry,' yelled one of the dwarfs. 'He'll be bloody dead by morning.' They stormed off into the night. We heard that a policeman was seen to be limping next day. But that night visit remained a rare shock of military reality breaking in on our oddly detached lives.

My letters home were always evasive about what I was actually doing on my 'Long day duties'. I limited myself to complaints about 'creeping out of bed in the frigid 4.55 a.m. darkness to wake up under the cold water tap'. We were unsure how far our mail was being checked by RAF censors, but it was obvious that detailed accounts of our activities would mean trouble. Not that there were thrilling yarns to be spun from the cycle of routine watches in the monitoring centre. The patterns were already embedded in our beings: 'Long days', 5 a.m. to 12.30, followed by 5 p.m. to midnight, 'Short days', 12.30 p.m. to 5 p.m., then a day off. 'Mids', the midnight to 8 a.m. shift, was especially unpopular. There were often piles of untranscribed tape recordings from the day shift to be logged, and we struggled to stay awake. The zombie state generated by the eternities in the darkened room did not tend to produce material for sparkling anecdotes. Struggling to fill a couple of pages, my letters are full of whiny self-dramatizings: 'At times like that I feel that all I need is a bed of straw, a scourge and a cowl to confirm my existence as an ascetic monk.' God knows what my parents made of that as they slogged away in the music shop.

It was probably as well they didn't know about my duties in the 'Direction Finding Tower'. In my letter home I made it sound like a jolly youth club outing: 'I managed to borrow a bike for riding to and from work. During the evening duty it was like riding around in a bottle of ice-cooled ink. About five times on the outward and three times on the return journey I found myself in ditches or in the middle of ploughed fields. I constantly felt that I was about to run into something large and furry which would carry me off into the darkness, bellowing with anger.' It reads like an unconscious pastiche of Christian's symbolic ordeals in *Pilgrim's Progress*. At the time, the ordeals of the DF Tower felt real enough.

The Direction Finding Tower was stuck out at the limits of RAF Gatow, hard up against the perimeter fence which was also the boundary of the Soviet Zone. Why it was decided to put the thing there, within sight of the watching troops and tanks of the Cold War enemy, was not for a nervous Linguist wobbling towards it on his bike to question. A couple of other Linguists had reported alarming encounters with the DF Tower.

One man was startled to find a hungry-looking face staring at him through the window late one night. Another man, cycling out in the dark, was shot at. I thought he was astonishingly sanguine about it. He said it must have been some drunken Russian soldier over the fence, but he didn't hang around to find out more. Edward said he was also used as target practice by a bored Russian soldier as he was clambering down the stairs at the end of his duty. 'I scuttled back up the steps and shut the light off,' he said. 'Then I pedalled for my life.'

We were all aware of just how close to the edge of the Iron Curtain were were at Gatow. We heard that the Army detachment on the base had admitted that they would not be able to hold off the Soviet troops for more than twenty minutes if they came through the fence. Still, sleeping so close to the enemy could have its lighter moments. I heard of an extraordinary incident when a couple of eighteen-year-old Soviet soldiers suddenly arrived one night at one of the Linguists' billets, begging for asylum. They had scrambled through the fence near the Direction Finding Tower and they were bleeding heavily. It appeared they had only just survived a mauling by their own killer dogs patrolling the fence. When they were asked why they had taken such a crazy risk, the desperate comrades replied: 'Because our officers wouldn't let us listen to Elvis Presley.'

Soon the order to head out for a duty to the DF Tower came my way. Pedalling away from the lights of the base into the black hole beyond the airstrip, I thought I could hear singing somewhere ahead of me.

A couple of minutes later, I was sure I could hear singing. I realized with a chill what it must be – the Soviet troops on the other side of the fence were trying to cheer themselves up with a few rousing choruses of 'My Little Tractor' or some other heartening favourite. For me, alone in the dark, it was anything but cheering. Just as I was considering what the punishment might be for turning back, I heard a plane approaching. Suddenly I was stabbed by a brilliant beam of light from overhead. It tracked me for a few yards, and then cut out to leave me in blackness again. Heart banging in my ears, feeling like an insect fleeing a swatter, I pedalled furiously towards a faint glimmer of a light. 'Please let it be the DF Tower,' I whimpered out loud. Then I spotted it, looming over me, a box on stilts. In my panic, I saw a Martian fighting machine from an overheated Hollywood version of *The War of the Worlds*. I dumped the bike and clattered up the stairs, pursued by the Red Army choir.

The man on duty looked glad to see me. 'Bloody singing,' he grunted. 'Here, you'd better see how this stupid thing is supposed to work.' He grasped a big flat wheel hanging from a spindle which disappeared through the roof. 'You spin this round, and when you think you hear the signal dip in the headphones, you press this ring and then write down the bearing.' He looked up and grinned. 'It's all balls.' Then he slapped me on the back and made his escape. I was on my own – just me and the Red Army.

For half an hour, I struggled with the rusty wheel. I heaved it round and round, straining to hear any variation in the level of the air traffic burbling through my headphones. I could detect no hint of a dip any-where. My sceptical instructor was right. The creaky device – no more than an aerial connected to a bike wheel – just didn't work. If the free world was relying on this pile of junk to deliver an early warning about the approach of the Red hordes, we were in a bad way. Meanwhile, the Soviet glee club was still belting away over the fence. They sounded drunk now.

So I gave up. What the hell, I had no sergeant looming over my shoulder, no one listening in on my frequency. The free world could do without my wonky intelligence for a while. I twiddled the radio tuner away from the Russian pilots and their dreary routines. Sud-denly, a bubbling Chet Baker solo flooded the hut, and then a voice, rich and reassuring. 'This is Willis Conover with the Voice of America Jazz Hour.' I turned up Chet, and drowned out the Russians.

It had been a trying evening. I thought it was better to spare my parents the details. I wrote: 'All in all, it was quite a relief to park the bike at midnight and stagger up to bed.'

Months later, Edward found out that our ordeals at the DF Tower were as pointless as I'd thought. All our bearings were bouncing off a metal building a few yards away inside RAF Gatow.

10

THE ROUTINES in the monitoring centre stretched before us in an eternity of scribbling. The Berlin winter had clamped down, making trips into the city an ordeal of numbed feet and frozen ears. I wrote home in what can only have been an ecstasy of boredom: 'The offer of a marquetry kit sounds most attractive. It would make a pleasant change from my interminable reading of the Cambridge History of English Literature, Volume One.' The prospect of toiling over a wooden picture of the Norfolk Broads or a Dutch windmill (complete with peasant and clogs) clearly filled me with a rare excitement after three months on the front line of the intelligence war.

By now, with my fellow Linguists, I had evolved an obsessive calculus to work out our remaining time in the RAF. After lengthy consultations with calendars, I estimated I still had 17,712,000 seconds to do. I consoled myself that it was 300,000 seconds less than at my last count. I contemplated trying to build a model of Leeds Town Hall out of matchsticks.

As young men chafing to get on with our lives, the

disaffection with military life – even a version of it as low on bull and bullshit as ours now was – is not hard to understand. If you add the fact that most of us were waiting to go to university, and were well supplied with the arrogance of the student and a snotty contempt for all things military, that fanatical countdown of seconds until escape was only to be expected. It felt like a vital ritual in the freemasonry of the 'civilians in uniform' we insisted we were. But most important of all, I think, in shaping our dissident culture were the daily frustrations of our jobs in the monitoring room.

We had quickly come to feel that we were little more than trainspotters, stranded on the sidelines scribbling down scraps of information while the Cold War Express thundered past to an unknown destination. On the rare occasions when something unusual cropped up in our headphones, like a personal exchange with a ground controller or a pilot in trouble, our logs were instantly snatched away and taken off into a back room for what was mysteriously called 'analysis'. A colleague logged the anguished final words of a pilot in trouble – 'I can't see anything,' the man was screaming – but that too was just more grist for the analysts. We had no knowledge of how our stuff might fit into a bigger picture, or what that bigger picture might be. We were not encouraged to ask.

Long after my National Service was over, a man who had been an officer in the Gatow monitoring centre gave me a glimpse of that bigger picture. Geoffrey Elliott had seen something of operations in those back rooms which had been a mystery to scribblers like me. He offered an intriguing insight about one destination for our material. 'We shared the daily traffic with the Americans,' Elliott said, 'and a courier would go over to our counterpart unit in Tempelhof airport and take the material.' One day the courier had not turned up, and Elliott was ordered to take the daily trawl across Berlin. 'It was an almost out-of-body experience,' he recalled, 'because they said, "Here's this extremely secret material, and the West would crumble if anyone got hold of it."' The nervous young Elliott was then handed a pistol and ammunition. 'There were six rounds wrapped in brown paper with red sealing wax at each end.' Elliott was told that if the sealing wax was broken, there would be a court of enquiry. 'I said: "Well, it's a little difficult, if someone does stop the car to say – wait a minute, while I unwrap this package and load my gun.' When he reached the American base, after negotiating a derelict flight of stairs, he found his way blocked by a huge steel door. Elliott felt defeated, as no one had mentioned the door or how to get past it. Luckily outside the door there was a Coca-Cola machine, and someone came out to get a Coke. He was able to follow the American and deliver his package. It was a surreal mix of tight and non-existent security which was so often a feature of my life as a spy.

The routines of those long days and nights with headphones and notepads, without any real understanding of what it was all for, inevitably generated a shared scepticism. I can't recall any of my fellow Linguists ever hinting at the notion that we were part of a grand struggle against the evils of Communism. Most of us were, like our parents, more inclined to be instinctively anti-American, disapproving of popular culture, more or less ignorant of politics. My own distaste for loud Americans and their unacceptable golfing trousers was of course confused by my worship of American jazz. Our take on the world was, I reckon, a low-level bloody-mindedness, barely leavened in our case by dollops of education. It's a kit of attitudes still celebrated today as basic British virtues.

The lack of knowledge about what we were really doing was of course fertile ground for the blossoming of lurid myths. In that pre-Christmas period, one Linguist swore he had heard through his headphones a merry voice with a Russian accent saying: 'A Happy Christmas to all our English listeners.' Then the Army Linguists in another section of the monitoring building claimed they had checked out some coordinates for the targeting of an artillery gun in the Soviet Zone, and had discovered it was aimed at our building.

But mostly, we tried to lose ourselves in a life beyond the headphones. In my room, while I got stuck into the joys of marquetry, Ron Akehurst brewed a foul-smelling cocktail of chemicals which he claimed would develop our films. There always seemed to be one ingredient missing. Dick Simms imbibed the local newspaper sent from home – the splendidly bucolic *Thrapston, Raunds and Oundle Journal* – and dreamed of his girlfriend. For the most part, the rest of us yearned, and I got on with the marquetry.

One Linguist claimed that he laid siege to a mysterious Stasi woman, 'But I never got anywhere,' he admitted. A bolder colleague, John – equipped with the brooding good looks of an urban Heathcliff – briefly gained a reputation as a successful gigolo. He brought back from his off-duty adventures torrid accounts of his cavortings in the lakeside forests with an alluring local fräulein. We listened and stirred with envy. Soon however, John's exploits became too public. He was called in for a word by the Wing-Commander, and the gigolo was grounded. It seems the threat to security and the possibility of pillow talk with the Gatow Mata Hari was too great to tolerate. What business she could have done selling the secrets of 'My undercarriage is down and locked' was not clear.

It is hard to recover now the pervasive sexual innocence and naïveté of that time and place. The vast majority of the Linguists were, I'm sure, like me, twenty-year-old virgins. We were inevitably loaded with overheated yearnings, but there was very little swapping of experiences or fantasies. Letters from the new girlfriend at home were filled with blameless gossip about friends or her drama group. And there was little in our surroundings to arouse us. Images in newspapers and magazines were limited to pretty girls in cardigans; the steamiest films imaginable, such as the notorious *And God Created Woman*, dared to show us Brigitte Bardot in a bikini and a pout. Advertising tended to feature housewives in aprons, or couples on bikes.

Racier stuff was confined to blush-inducing nudist magazines. *Health and Efficiency*, which sounded like a bracing Hitler Youth tract, introduced generations of puzzled young men to the geography of naked women.

It was hardly an arousing peepshow. For page after page, cheery women nudists frolicked at volleyball, or stood smiling in cornfields. All of them sported mysterious cloudy bits below the waist. For most youths of my time, the only access to less decorous visions of the unadorned female form was via *National Geographic* magazine. Well-thumbed back numbers, tracked down in doctors' and dentists' waiting-rooms, provided occasional glimpses of topless Trobriand Islanders, or naked Kayapo Indians in the Brazilian rainforests. The lesson seemed to be that non-white women were fair game for our fevered fantasies.

Meanwhile, at RAF Gatow, we looked forward to a Bavarian evening at the camp social club as a pre-Christmas revel – 'Best uniforms and white shirts required.' As I wrote excitedly to my parents in anticipation: 'Bavarian evening conjures up entrancing visions of sunburned old men in leather shorts coming to the doorway with an accordion to bid a cheery welcome.' The reality, after a slither through the snow, was a big empty hall with a few logs nailed to the wall. Still, there was a man with an accordion – though I am to this day very much of my father's opinion that a gentleman is a chap who knows how to play the accordion, and doesn't.

But then people began to pour in and things started to warm up. I won a holdall in a raffle, but, even more thrilling, my friend Stu won a monster Christmas hamper. I even managed a shuffling sort of dance with a girl wearing huge glasses. But the spirit of the evening – more Billy Bunter, I fancy, than Andy Warhol – was conveyed in the excited letter I wrote to my parents: 'There were tables laden with jellies, cream cake, salads, pies . . . and all free for the taking! Everyone filled their plates with an appalling mixture of salad cream on jelly, sausage pies with cream cake, and tucked in voraciously. After eleven pm things began to get really hectic. There was an RAF Police Corporal reeling all over the place with four candles burning on the edge of his plate of food, unsteadily lighting everyone's cigarette (No, not mine, Mum, fear not!)'

The demon tobacco was a particular horror for my mother. My father had always smoked heavily, and she never tired of lamenting it. Of course it had no effect, and my father carried on happily with his sixty-a-day habit, leaving his expired butts like the tracks of a prowling bear. I was never sure whether her objections were moral, financial or medical. I suspect the fact that everything in the house, including her husband, was marinated in tobacco smoke might have been the real reason. Whatever it was, I picked up her distaste and never even experimented with a gasper.

By chance, the Bavarian evening was preserved in a snap. I still have it, a tipsy picture of a group posed behind a table full of drained glasses. The girl with specs is there, next to a grinning officer with a crooked bow tie. A dozen of my half-forgotten chums crowd round, all visibly the worse for wear. On the front row is a young airman with an uncertain smile, looking unfittingly sober. Me.

My report home concluded: 'I decided that I'd better take my room-mate back to our room. He seemed to conceive a sudden unguarded scorn of authority on the totter back towards the block, and insisted on bellowing rather uncomplimentary comments into the night about several high-ranking officials of our acquaintance. Fortunately they were hardly likely to be strolling around camp at midnight to take offence, so I finally got him back without trouble. Quite an evening.'

A couple of nights later, I was asked by a Sergeant if I would babysit for him and his wife at their house on the base. As they left for whatever limited revels were available in the area, the Sergeant motioned to his well-stocked drinks cabinet. 'Help yourself, if you fancy a drink,' he said. An hour into my watch over the sleeping baby, I suddenly decided to go for it. I poured myself a gin and orange, trying to shrug off the spectre of my teetotal, pub-shunning parents. With the abandon of the novice more accustomed to tumblers of lemonade, I poured a lot of gin and not much orange. It tasted odd, I thought, but rather nice. I poured myself another.

By the time the Sergeant and his wife got home, I was drunk for the first time in my life. I was in a spinning room, struggling to preserve the impression that I could stand up. I made a speedy exit and reeled off down the interminable road towards my billet. After a few yards, I was comprehensively sick. Fumbling my way into bed, I thought maybe my parents were right about the demon drink. Maybe.

11

IN THE DAYS before Christmas 1957, things seemed to be looking up a bit. I'd been provisioned by a vast food parcel from home – Mackintosh's Quality Street misshapes (factory rejects, made in Halifax), four tins of mixed nuts, a jar of bottled chicken, ten Mars bars, apples, pear drops, aniseed balls, lemonade powder. Then there was Stu's raffle prize hamper (funny German sausages, cherries in wine, ham, sweet buns). So there would at least be a festive break from the sludgy stuff served up in the canteen. Food had never been a particular interest for me, but the gulag glop of mashed potatoes and pulverized stew on offer at the end of the cookhouse queues had managed to dismay even my palate. Like me, my fellow Linguists were wartime kids. For years, bananas and oranges were things we read about in stories; after the war, rationing left many of us on a regular diet of dried potatoes, powdered egg and horsemeat – with the occasional tin of peaches as a delicacy. Now the prospect of a blowout Christmas in the billet was greeted with the excitement of toddlers waiting for Santa.

Just before Christmas, I went foraging. My two days

off coincided with the weekend, and along with a few other bold spirits I grappled with the underground map. We headed off across the city into the American Sector of Berlin, determined to get as far away from those Russian pilots as possible. Heady with seasonal spirit, in a shop near the Schoenberg S-Bahn station, I spotted a jar of caviar, the first I'd ever seen. I bought it. Peering through the glass, I thought it looked like ball-bearings in axle grease.

Down the street, a cinema was showing some stupid film about Las Vegas. We piled in, abandoning our undergraduate sneers at the door. It was bliss, banishing for a while the bleakness of Cold War Berlin. Full of girls and sunshine, noisy, pointless and hugely enjoyable, the film reminded me of all my favourite fantasies about America. For an hour, I forgot my routine prejudices about the Yanks. After all, the only recurring dream I'd ever had was about sailing into New York harbour on the *Queen Elizabeth*. My jazz heroes lived in America, in a never-never land of skyscrapers and palm trees. Gene Kelly danced through the streets, and everything was in Technicolor.

My crude movie poster vision of the American dream was, I guess, shared by most of my generation in the monochrome Europe of the 1950s. It was only thirty years later when I went to Russia that I discovered our Cold War enemies had the same yearning. Sickened by the nonstop barrage of Soviet propaganda and the drabness of daily life, people from Moscow to Vladivostok looked at state TV reports droning on about poverty and inequality in America. Then they turned down the hectoring commentaries, and gazed longingly at the shop windows in the background. Denied the seditious messages of US rock 'n' roll, they made bootleg copies of Chubby Checker's 'Let's Twist Again' on Uncle Oleg's X-ray plates, and smuggled them to nervous buyers in doorways off Red Square. A Moscow friend told me he became obsessed with bootlegged Beach Boys records and combed his English dictionaries for the meaning of 'surfin''. Not finding it, he became convinced it must mean 'fucking'.

Of course, even Cold War Berlin was a lot more fun than Moscow. But for a while in the cinema, I bathed in that warm American fantasy set in the Nevada desert.

Out on the Berlin street in a steady drizzle, the celluloid Las Vegas was instantly sluiced away. None of us was ready to head back to base. 'Why don't we try that place?' Ivor suggested, jerking a thumb at a seedy-looking doorway under a sign which flickered the name 'Eierschale'. 'Eggshell, I think,' said Stu. 'OK, let's see what's down there.' Under the glare of a suspicious-looking girl, we headed down a narrow flight of stairs.

I couldn't ever remember seeing so many human beings crammed into so small a space. A warren of cellars stretched into the gloom, people glued together by a trad jazz band belting out 'Muskrat Blues'. It was very hot and hard to move, and I loved it.

I felt suddenly shaken awake, after months of suspended animation in the routines of the monitoring centre. It seemed that the life of a National Service spy, far from galvanizing me with risk and danger, had sent me into hibernation, curled up inside my headphones.

Via snatches of conversation yelled through the uproar, we gathered that many of the crowd were students from Berlin University. Flaunting beards and jeans, they declared their membership of the Beat Generation. We were a long way from Manhattan, but these people seemed pretty wild to me. I had never encountered such eccentrics. My God, didn't that girl over there even have her jumper on back to front !

If I had any ideas about spying on the local counter-culture, my disguise was instantly rumbled. As I goggled at the spectacle of Berlin's bohemia, a bearded youth looked me up and down. 'You must be English,' he said in impeccable English. 'I can tell by your shoes and trousers and sweater and shirt and tie.'

The tie. I can still recall the embarrassment of that tie in the Eierschale. I hoped the gloom hid my blushes. The beard was very nice about it, but I knew he was amused to meet someone so comically English – and so entrancingly square. This was a place unguessed at by the church youth club in Halifax, where a disputed point on the badminton court was about as wild as it got. And these were people who were grabbing lives I could hardly imagine. It seemed like it might be fun.

The band roared into another trad favourite, the inevitable 'Saints Go Marchin' In'. They were good though, and the beat drove up through my feet. That jazz cellar in 50s Berlin woke me up to the possibilities of a life after National Service, even perhaps a life after Halifax.

On Christmas Day in our room, we opened the jar of caviar. We thought it tasted queer.

12

THE FIRST DAYS OF 1958 were an obstacle course, skidding over rain-lubricated sheets of ice. I ended my four-day Christmas break with a shopping trip in the city – nylons for Cousin Margaret, slippers (pink!) for my mother. But despite the dispiriting weather, I felt almost happy for the first time in Berlin. Maybe it was that glimpse of something different at the Eierschale; maybe it was the sense I had turned a corner, into the final months of National Service.

Even the work in the monitoring centre had a new spark. It was suddenly much more intensive, long days with torrents of communications traffic to report. The marquetry languished. In my letters home, I found myself reporting: 'I don't think I've ever slogged as hard since I came out here, but surprisingly enough I've enjoyed it. So perhaps I'm not completely a lost hope as far as work is concerned, and there's some chance of shaking off service indolence when I become a free man.'

Feeling more confident now about exploring the city, I spent days off nosing about in unfamiliar districts. With a couple of adventurous colleagues, I tramped around the French Sector, and had a meal in the French Services Centre. We braced ourselves and, feeling supremely bold, ordered the frogs' legs. More edible than the caviar, I thought.

THE CRUDE carving-up of Berlin at Potsdam after the war had left ragged edges. Several Soviet memorials were stranded in Allied territory, one of them on the British side of the Brandenburg Gate. The monument to the Fallen Heroes of the Motherland was put together within weeks of the Allied victory from the remnants of the Nazi Reichs Chancellery. Flanked by two Soviet T-34 tanks, the first to enter the city as the Red Army swept in, it marked the point where the battle for Berlin had been won.

This splendid piece of Communist kitsch was the site of one of the most haunting memories of my time in Berlin. With Ivor and Ron, I walked through the Tiergarten on a raw afternoon to have a look at the memorial. As we got closer, we could see that a couple of Soviet soldiers were guarding the thing, stamping their feet against the cold. In fact their comrades were to continue goose-stepping up and down in front of the memorial for the next thirty years, as the Berlin Wall rose and fell only yards away.

That afternoon, one of the soldiers stood to attention near us, impossibly young and shivering and a long way from home. 'I'm going to have a word,' Ivor announced. We walked up to the chap. He looked about fifteen. The Red Menace shrivelled to a kid in a crumpled uniform with cracked boots. Summoning up his nonmilitary Russian, Ivor ventured, 'How are you?' The kid glanced at us. After a moment he said, 'Where am I?' Ron told him, 'Berlin.' 'What's that?' the kid asked. 'Germany,' I said. He looked puzzled. Then he said, 'Where's Germany?'

An officer bustled up and marched the kid off. We walked back down Strasse dem 17 Juli and found a bar. We had several beers.

A couple of weeks later, I decided it was time to take a trip into Soviet East Berlin. It was three years before the Wall would slice through the city, and travel in and out of the Communist-controlled sector of the city was still possible. In 1958, in fact, 75,000 underground, bus and tram tickets were sold every day in the West to people from the East. Twelve thousand schoolchildren from the East went to school in the West. Every week, 5,000 East German refugees were fleeing through Berlin, joining the ominous tide of defections which would soon drive the regime to seal their country behind a wall they called an 'anti-fascist protective measure'.

I had heard hair-raising stories of a Linguist who strayed into East Berlin and was picked up by the Stasi. Imprisoned for months, he used his time in the exercise yard to memorize the names of the other British servicemen he met who were being held by the East Germans. When he was finally released, the JSSL man was able to give RAF security a full list. He got a letter of commendation, but I felt I could do without that experience.

With the alarms still fresh in my memory about the risks to Linguists of getting tangled up with East German security police, I opted for an official bus trip.

Even the bus, I had heard from other Linguists, some-times had to run the gauntlet of furious East Berlin citizens. Enraged by memories of Allied bombing or by Soviet scare stories, the buses returned from some trips to the East smeared with the spittle of hostile pedes-trians. Leaving behind my RAF uniform with its telltale inverted stripe, I donned my Cambridge blazer as a talisman against the Commies.

From the safe capsule of the coach, passing through the Brandenburg Gate was still an unsettling experience. Over the months I had been in Berlin, this had always marked the end of my world, the portal to a dangerous and frightening empire stretching all the way to the edge of the vast Soviet Union. If the mythic 'Iron Curtain', coined by Churchill a decade earlier, had a physical existence, it had to be here. Before long, of course, it would be made hideously real in the shape of the Berlin Wall; but years before the concrete and barbed-wire fact of the Wall imprisoned millions of East Germans, the border with the Soviet Sector of the city was a dead zone. Now I was on the other side, in enemy territory.

The bus took us first on a pilgrimage to the colossal Soviet Memorial in Treptower Park, an awesome pile of Communist heroics. The East German tour organizers were determined that we should understand the enor-mous sacrifices of the Soviet soldiers who had liberated the city. I gaped at the forty-foot-high statue of a Red Army soldier, carved out of red marble plundered from Hitler's Chancellery. I took a photo of the giant, a baby in one arm, a sword on the other, his foot grinding a broken swastika. The war felt very close. My guidebook told me the park had been the scene of a huge Communist demonstration before World War I. It also recounted the terrible battle for Berlin in April 1945, when the Soviet army entered to city to find the bodies of the Nazis' German opposition hanging from lampposts. Five thousand men, a fraction of the number of Soviet soldiers who had died in the struggle for the city, were buried in the park. A massive statue of Mother Russia loomed over the place, carved from a single piece of granite intended for a Nazi victory arch.

I remembered grey Sunday afternoons in Yorkshire with my grandmother, patrolling the cemetery where squads of her distant relatives were buried. The old lady seemed to relish it, pausing for ages to read the headstones and pass judgement on the state of the flowers. It was an essential West Riding Sunday ritual, to be fitted in between chapel and high tea. I used to think I was just very bored in a stoical northern way. I reckon 'desperate' might have been nearer the mark. In Treptower Park that afternoon, chilled by the weight of all this history and all this grief, I couldn't wait to escape to the tour bus.

After the war, the Soviet Union had ruled East Germany directly. Stalin demanded punitive German reparations and the East had to pay them, stripping its industries. In 1949, the satellite 'German Democratic Republic' was put in place – a one-party state, ruled by exiled Communists brought back from Mother Russia and policed by the Stasi, 'the shield and sword of the Communist Party'. The Russian masters had then plundered East Germany's production, leaving the country

impoverished and resentful. I had read something about
the East Berlin uprising of June 1953, when workers'
demonstrations and riots had threatened the existence
of the Communist regime. East Germans had shouted
'Death to Communism' and even 'Long live Eisenhower'. Erupting just three months after the death of
Stalin, and spreading to hundreds of cities, towns and
villages, it had been the first violent rebellion in the
Communist bloc. It had taken Soviet tanks to stamp out
the uprising, and it left the Communist government
pathologically suspicious of its own people. Looking
out of the bus window, it was not hard to see what
had fuelled the despairing rage of the demonstrators.

The spectacle of the other Berlin stunned me. This
was a journey into a ruined landscape. A dozen years
after the war, uncleared rubble still lined some streets.
Many buildings remained pock-marked by the shells of
the liberating armies of 1945. The few wretched roadside
stalls looked almost bare of things to buy. Dispirited-
looking people trudged along, hauling their kids. I saw a
family trundling their belongings in an old pram, like
refugees fleeing a battle. There were police with dogs,
and soldiers everywhere. It was hard to believe the
shining shops just minutes away on the Kurfürstendamm
were in the same universe.

The bus trip into East Berlin was my first collision
with that other reality made by Communism, and the
beginning of an obsession. We crossed the windy spaces
of the Alexanderplatz, with its slogans extolling Lenin
and the Party and the Five Year Plan. The guide told us
we were coming up to 'Stalinallee', and declared it was

'the showcase of Socialist progress'. I grabbed a snap through the bus window. That photo has frozen my memory of the place. Under a featureless grey sky, a grey road runs without deviation to a murky vanishing point. On both sides, identical grey buildings, regular as the bricks they're built from, march down the road. There is almost no one to be seen.

The BBC TV version of Orwell's *Nineteen Eighty-Four* was still fresh in my memory. The vision of a totalitarian nightmare had stunned millions of viewers when it was shown only three years earlier. The play had aroused a storm of criticism. There were motions in Parliament, and press claims that a viewer had died of shock. I had watched it with my parents, and had been horrified by the unremitting bleakness of the world it described. But I had filed it away as a fable. Now I felt I was driving into the reality of that vision.

The bus turned down a side street to head back west. Abruptly, Stalinallee was revealed to be a fantasy. Seen from behind, the 'Socialist showcase' looked more like a tacky theatre set. Propping up the stern and substantial-seeming facade was a tangle of wooden scaffolding. Behind that was a wilderness of weed-strewn rubble.

I was hooked. Something about the absurdity and otherness of the East grabbed me instantly. I was appalled by it, but it stuck to me. It took me years to have an idea of why I became addicted. Perhaps the grimness felt like some kind of replay of Halifax just after the war, the gloom, the empty shops, the restrictions, the habits of obedience. But this time I had an escape. I didn't live here. I could be a tourist in the theme park of my own remembered boyhood. I could dip into a Socialist version of life on Market Balcony – and then get out.

As my tour bus rolled back through the Brandenburg Gate and into the British Sector after that first brief encounter with the awfulness of life in a Soviet satellite, it felt like coming home. But I knew I'd be going back.

13

THE MODERN JAZZ QUARTET were coming to play a concert in Berlin. I found a chum who would stand in for my evening duty, and filled in the wearisome official forms which would let me out of the cage for a few hours. It would be a thrilling consolation for the fact that a concert advertised in the base cinema had just been cancelled: 'California's Sweetheart of Song' and 'The Pin-up Girl' would not be coming to entertain us after all. Maybe the fact that Pin-up Girl's publicity photo had been nicked by lecherous hands from a board outside the canteen had scared her off. I felt I could live with the disappointment.

I had loved the MJQ ever since, as a newly jazz-obsessed teenager, I had come upon a bright yellow extended-play record in my parents' stock. Shutting myself away with the exquisitely poised cocktail of vibraphone, piano, bass and drums, I got lost in the music. Even via my tinny little Dansette record player, it sounded sublime. But like all my jazz heroes, the MJQ had always seemed to live in another galaxy.

Now they were here, on the other side of the city of

course, but within reach. I pored over a detailed map of Berlin and eventually found the place tucked away deep in the American Sector. Crushed into an impossibly crowded bus with a couple of Linguist pals, I realized I had no idea where to get off. We decided to follow the likeliest-looking passengers, the ones in the beat outfits of duffle coats and sandals. At last, with only minutes to go before the start of the concert, the tribe led off into the night.

The Kongress Halle was a startling vision of the new West Berlin. Looming up out of the darkness, a dream of glass and light, after my recent experience of the other Berlin it seemed designed to be a mocking declaration of superiority. I thought the MJQ were the perfect complement to the place, restrained yet thrilling. Even a lengthy introduction by some German smart arse in a suit – probably 'Herr Doctor Jazz', we decided – failed to dim my rapture.

Six months in, like my colleagues I was at last sucking some juice out of being in Berlin. Some of my comrades had managed to set themselves up with occasional jobs. Mike told me he was teaching English to a widow – 'with extras', he said. Other Linguists were overdosing on classical concerts and opera, relishing performances of Wagner's Ring Cycle and *Der Rosenkavalier*. They were also piling up Supraphon LPs, bought at the Czech House of Culture in the Alexanderplatz for a few throwaway Ostmarks. Others risked joining an audience in East Berlin largely made up of Soviet officers for a performance of *Eugene Onegin*. To me, that sounded more like a punishment than a treat.

I heard about one adventurous Linguist just before my time who regularly hauled his alto sax into East Berlin to play in a jazz group along with a couple of sons of Socialism. I shudder to imagine how the military would have responded if they'd known about it. Such flagrant fraternizing with the Cold War enemy would have been severely dealt with.

In fact Berlin seemed to be becoming something of a jazz Mecca. Perhaps because a Musicians' Union embargo prevented most American jazzmen from playing in Britain, they were trekking out regularly to play gigs on the edge of the free world. Only a few weeks after my MJQ treat, I was offered another jazz banquet: 'The Jazz West Coast Show' – my ultimate consolation prize for the months of being marooned in Berlin.

I'm not sure why the West Coast jazz of the 1950s became such a passion for me, but it had to do with the coming of LPs. My father came back from a record-ordering trip in Manchester enthusing about a new miracle he'd seen called 'long-playing records'. Soon the new LPs began to make it to Halifax, decked out in their seductive covers. Now the clunky old 78s in their brown paper bags felt like leftovers from the war. Before long, gramophone needles, once a staple item in my mother's record shop, were consigned to antique stalls and museums.

It must have been in 1953, mooning around in the record shop, that I came upon an LP by the Gerry Mulligan Quartet. It wasn't love at first hearing. The harmonies of Mulligan's gruff baritone sax and Chet Baker's wispy trumpet sounded odd to a fifteen-year-old, entirely innocent of jazz or jazz people. Soon, though, I was addicted. I played the haunting tracks over and over, somehow feeling the noise of it, silky and seductive, slide inside me. I hijacked more Mulligan Quartet records from the shop, and then moved out to trawl other bands and people who were making that special sound. I devoured sleeve notes and tracked down articles. I lost myself in Steve Race's jazz record programme on the BBC Home Service. I discovered there was a music called West Coast, and that it happened in and around Los Angeles, in the dreamscape of Southern California. Most of it seemed to be recorded by a label called Pacific Jazz. Indulged by my parents, who were probably relieved that I'd found something to engage with, I quickly built up a collection. In my imagination, I explored the miraculous places pictured on the LP covers, the backdrops for musicians awkwardly clutching trumpets and saxophones on beaches, or hanging on to yachts, or cruising along multi-lane freeways in open-top cars.

This far off neverland inhabited by its exotic tribe of musicmakers became my ultimate teenage crush. It had everything I needed at that moment. It felt exclusive – for a while I didn't know anyone who had ever heard of it – and it was happening in a golden place far away. With its tendency to pretentious flirtations with classical influences – experimenting with French horns and oboes and flutes – the music also gratified my unformed egghead inclinations. Ultimately, I guess West Coast was, for a timid teenager, a safe adventure. I wasn't ready for all the raw emotion of the fierce bebop I had heard, the jazz of Charlie Parker and Dizzy Gillespie. And of course, though I can't remember thinking about it at the time, bebop was black while West Coast was essentially white. The BBC Home Service spared its listeners the untidy details of the desperate drug habits and chaotic lives of my West Coast heroes.

Now West Coast was coming to Berlin. Those same jazzmen – Bud Shank, Bob Cooper, Claude Williamson – had stepped out of my record covers and were within reach. The venue for the concert was decidedly un-Californian. The vast Sportpalast looked more like an arena for a six-day cycle race than a concert hall. Apparently it had a been a favourite venue for Hitler's rantings. Still, even in this unpromising place, my heroes did not let me down. The flute and oboe duets of Shank and Cooper curled around me for a couple of hours, warming me with a dose of Californian sunshine for days afterwards as I battled with a streaming cold and a Berlin winter which felt never ending.

In the early spring of 1958, I could almost believe the jazz visitors had somehow opened a tunnel between my squad of Berlin-marooned Linguists and the outside world. My friend Stu was due to escape for home leave in Huddersfield, though rumours of a West German transport strike left him in an agony of uncertainty. We heard that Elvis was swapping his guitar for a rifle and heading for military service in Germany. I wrote home to gloat: 'So that puts me one up on Elvis, with exactly a hundred days to do. I wouldn't swap positions with him for every dollar he's amassed. Once you're in the Services, your wealth is only reckoned in how little you have to do before demob. By those standards, I'm a millionaire, while Elvis is a wretched pauper.'

We even had a visit from the Minister of Defence. The news that Mr Duncan Sandys was coming for a day trip to RAF Gatow filled us with dread. The potential for a panicky campaign of spit and polish loomed over us for days. Awful visions of basic training, and the lunacies of glazed toecaps, squared-up socks and white-washed coal heaps, stirred in the collective memory. In the event we Linguists were spared, probably because our military masters despaired of getting their scruffy eggheads up to scratch in the time available. Happily, the 'poison dwarfs' of the Inniskilling Regiment were ready to step into the breach, resplendent in white webbing and shining rifles, fully equipped with bellow-ing Sergeant-Majors. Surprisingly, a few of us off-duty Linguists were allowed to stroll down to the airstrip to watch the spectacle and take snaps.

A sleek Comet jetliner touched down, an Army band struck up, Army officers of steepling rank strutted and preened. Military police with uniforms creased like card-board boxes observed me and my shabby chums with impotent loathing. The Minister descended among us from his Comet, our shutters clicked. After a cursory inspection of the immaculate Inniskillings, the import-ant visitor was whisked away in a convoy of black limousines.

I suspect now that there must have been more to that visit than a bit of Ruritanian spectacle. It was off my primitive political radar at the time, but the timing of the Minister's trip may well have had to do with the threat of Sputnik, and the sudden prospect of Soviet missiles. Sandys had recently been responsible for a highly controversial initiative to cancel almost all military aircraft development in favour of missiles.

His arrival in Berlin coincided with a brisk upswing in the spying trade. Prime Minister Anthony Eden, who had been destroyed by the débâcle of Britain's abortive Suez invasion, had cancelled many espionage operations, fearful of provoking the Soviet enemy. The death of a Royal Navy diver who had been spying on a Soviet cruiser during a visit to Britain by the Communist leadership also left Eden uneasy about espionage operations – particularly as the diver's headless and handless body had washed up shortly after the departure of his Soviet guests.

Now the new Prime Minister, Harold Macmillan, was putting a fresh energy behind the effort to watch what the Soviets were up to. He had reactivated flights from Britain by U-2 spy planes, as well as photo and electronic surveillance of Soviet ships. At the same time, in Moscow, Nikita Khrushchev was blustering that the Soviet Union was turning out missiles like sausages. And he was once again racking up the tension by interfering with the passage of military trains through East Germany into Berlin.

For all my flirtations with caviar, frogs' legs and jazz, I was still in the front line of the Cold War.

14

'Dear Mum and Dad,
    Big news this week was – we have Spring.'

AFTER THE ENDLESS Berlin winter, it felt like a reprieve from an unearned prison sentence. On Sunday afternoon, a few of us went for a stroll by the lake near the base. Only the other day it had been a sheet of ice, a few old men shuffling around, muffled up to the eyes. Now it was crowded with Berliners messing about in summerhouses and boats. Even the Cold War seemed to have thawed for a moment.

Best of all, I was summoned for my pre-release medical examination. In the waiting-room, leafing through tattered old RAF magazines, I found a gem of a letter. 'Whenever I go out with my girlfriend, she insists I wear my RAF uniform as I look smarter in it than in my civvies. She dotes on that uniform. I'm afraid of what's going to happen when I'm demobbed. I don't want to sign on for good, but had I better do that to keep her love for me?' I filed that in my 'Would you believe it?' collection, alongside the creepy airman who requested *Family Favourites* to play the 'RAF March' for his commanding officer.

As I waited for the medical officer, I recalled the check-up before I began National Service. I found my way to a dusty church hall in Bradford, taking my place alongside a row of mournful youths. I had heard stories about brave souls who had tried to prove their unfitness for military service by eating soap. Apparently it could increase your heart rate to danger level for a few minutes and fool the doctor. I suspected that it would just make me foam at the mouth and get me arrested. Anyway, this was Yorkshire in the 1950s, not the Vietnam draft. Like the rest, I submitted to a bit of desultory prodding and was pronounced 'A1'. No escape, not even the cherished flat-feet get-out of 'excused boots'.

But the pre-release medical was something else. I welcomed it as a stepping-stone on my journey to freedom, and I walked into the examination room with a spring in my stride. A few minutes later I reeled out, only slightly dented by the invasion of my ears. The medic had pronounced me fit – 'apart from a bit of waxy build-up in the ears'. The waxy ears were a thing I had occasionally suffered since childhood. They had been the source of a bizarre exploration by a doctor during a wartime air-raid. There was a blackout, so we were forbidden to turn on any lights in the house. I've never forgotten how that doctor peered into my ear with the aid of a toy military searchlight mounted on the back of a truck which my father had made for me. The RAF medic produced an equally unsettling implement – a syringe the size of a small fire extinguisher. He opened the window and aimed a trial squirt into the bushes. I noted with alarm that it rattled the leaves across the road. The thing sluiced into my ear with the force of a high-pressure hose and the roar of an express train. The birds sounded deafening as I walked back to the monitoring building.

Strolling into work an hour late, I was pounced on by Warrant Officer Durrant. 'Where've you been then, lad?' he hissed. 'A medical, sir,' I said, and then with a barely suppressed smirk, 'A pre-release medical.' I briefly enjoyed the notion that his pre-release medical wouldn't be due for eighteen years. But he had his counter-attack ready – the grim news that we were getting so busy now that all leave might well be cancelled.

I had been thinking for months about the prospect of leave and how to use it. I wondered about going home, but now that I was in sight of demob, that seemed rather pointless. I had a half-formed notion about grabbing the chance to see something of the world outside the Berlin straitjacket, but where – and how? Paris seemed horribly expensive, and likely to wipe out most of the savings I had been squirrelling away via postal orders in letters home: 'Here's another £3 for the Natwest coffers.' Austria, Germany, Switzerland . . .

Tales of epic wanderings by JSSL people on leave breaks had become legendary. I heard about one pair of Linguists who set out to hitch lifts on RAF flights back home. Slogging through a frustrating maze of cancelled flights, broken planes and dodgy information, they trudged between bases in Cyprus, Turkey, Greece, Italy and Malta. It took them three weeks to get home, and then they had to turn round instantly to get back before their leave expired.

A few fortunates even managed to escape Berlin on duty. Phil and a couple of pals were ordered to head off to Lübeck after a plane was shot down. It was decided there might be 'repercussions' and it would be important to have some Linguists in the area who might pick up useful radio traffic. 'In fact,' Phil recalled with a dreamy smile, 'there was absolutely nothing to do – but lots to drink.' Immediately after they got back to Gatow, Phil and his lucky chums were sent off to the Harz Mountains in the expectation of debriefing Russian refugees. Again, nothing happened. 'It took us four days to drink the camp dry,' Phil reported.

Now it looked as if I was stuck in Berlin for the duration. I had to admit that the Warrant Officer was right. The workload in the monitoring centre was approaching breaking point. We had been told to expect a new intake of Linguist serfs for weeks, but they seemed to have got lost somewhere between Crail, Pucklechurch and Berlin. All the frequencies were loaded with traffic, all of us were feeling punch drunk. In a brief break, I saw *Bridge on the River Kwai* and identified totally with the wretched servicemen slogging away on that bridge. We didn't have Alec Guinness to keep our chins up, but I consoled myself with the certainty that the days were draining away towards my release. My uniform, shiny and almost see-through in places, was like a worn-out sofa. I hoped it would last out, or I might be faced with the unthinkable demand that I pay for a replacement. I performed small miracles of transplant surgery, snipping out linings and grafting them on to fraying regions of the crotch area.

My parents wrote to tell me they had spotted Sputniks One and Two passing over Halifax. I was tickled by the idea of the space dog Laika peering down on Market Balcony from its berth on Sputnik Two. But the unchallenged Soviet command of space was alarming the Western Allies and putting a real chill on the Cold War.

Even from my very humble niche in the espionage trade, I had an inkling of how this could impact on our working hours. Until now, the crazy calculations of Mutually Assured Destruction had allowed the nervous Allies to count on several days' warning of a Soviet strike. Any build-up of enemy ground forces gathering to invade the West would be spotted, defences could be alerted. The new reality of living under the shadow of Sputnik and its successors, armed perhaps with weapons to rain down death and destruction, had suddenly shrivelled that warning time to almost nothing. To ratchet up the paranoia, most American attempts to launch their own satellite seemed to be collapsing in a farcical sequence of launch-pad damp squibs. 'Flopniks', the press called them.

There was obviously a new and more pressing need to know what the Soviets might do. Western Intelligence had repeatedly under-estimated Soviet capabilities. After World War II, British Intelligence was convinced that it would be ten years before Moscow could contemplate another war. The first Soviet atomic test in 1949 exploded Western complacency. Again, during the Korean War, the sudden appearance of the MiG-15 fighter plane had shocked Western analysts. Now, we had Sputnik. And Mr Khrushchev was making noises about ending the Four Power Agreement and handing over Berlin to the East German Communists.

For me, the new tensions meant weeks of night duty. I became a creature of the night, slumping over my radio in the monitoring room, listening and scribbling and trying not to nod off. Sometimes we got lucky and the Sergeant on duty would actually make us cups of tea. One night, I watched him sweeping up carefully so as not to wake a chum who had fallen asleep at his post. When the air traffic was light in the small hours, this saint in blue allowed us to escape for a few minutes' respite with the British Forces Network radio. I usually found the announcers so infuriatingly jolly at 3 a.m. that even the limited appeal of some MiG circling around in the dark could claim me back. The BFN signoff – 'Auf wieder-cheers!' – was the last straw.

At last, in mid-May, we got our new intake – four fresh-faced Linguists, hot from training. We had hoped for twenty. But the ban on leave was suspended, which meant I might be able to escape for a few days.

15

IN THE BRIEF RESPITE provided by our four new arrivals, there was a collective rush for the door. The prospect of getting out of our triple-barred cage – monitoring centre, RAF Gatow, Berlin – generated a mild delirium. Over an impromptu banquet of chicken and banana rolls, tinned pineapple and trifle served in tin lids and mugs, we traded wild ideas about where to go for leave. After all the delays and cancellations, it was too late now for me to get a passport. Paris had slipped away. With Ivor, I pored over a map, fantasizing about what we might do with our nine days of freedom and RAF border visas.

My room-mate Dick was hoping to make a break for home. There was the steady girlfriend back there amid the Northamptonshire mangel-wurzels, and besides, he had months more remaining National Service to do than me. Dick planned to try to hitch a lift on an RAF plane which made the trip from Gatow to the UK every week. It would mean completing a stack of forms and surviving a grilling interview. Even if he came through all that, he knew that at any moment up to takeoff he might have to surrender his seat to any officer who fancied a trip to Blighty. This casual theft of your seat could also happen on the return trip. Then Dick would have to pay for his own fare back to Berlin, plus face a serious charge of being absent without leave. Despite the hazards, he seemed resolute. But then Dick always had the placid determination of the English yeoman. 'It would be nice to have actually flown while I'm in the Air Force,' he said.

Ivor jabbed a finger at the map. 'Innsbruck,' he said, 'let's go to Innsbruck.' As it happened, I had been there once, passing through on a school trip. I had fond memories of delicious apple juice in a pavement café and a spectacular cable car. It wasn't exactly the promise of sultry girls, drugs and debauchery which awaited Vietnam soldiers on R & R a decade later. But this was 1958. We agreed on Innsbruck.

In the two weeks before my leave was due, work built up to to the level of apoplexy. It seemed the Soviets were throwing everything into the sky in an effort to drain us and our stocks of carbon paper. After eight months of incessant listening and scribbling, we were all weary and jaded. Still, I would soon be sipping that apple juice on the pavements of Innsbruck . . .

Holidays had never been much of an event in my life up to then. During World War II, the occasional day trip to Loch Lomond had usually been the most exotic thing available. Just once, there was an adventurous few days in wartime Blackpool, sharing a boarding-house with a group of Canadian airmen. I had found myself surrounded by a tribe of laughing giants and adopted as a mascot, bringing a hint of transatlantic good times to the blacked-out resort. In post-war Halifax, the music shop ruled our lives and rationed our holidays. My father felt the shop should never be closed on a Saturday. That meant our longest holiday was four days – usually a quick dash to Redcar on the north Yorkshire coast. The steel works of Middlesbrough loomed at the end of the beach, and I felt we had somehow dragged the grim industrial landscape of home along with us.

But now, in Berlin, I could plan my own holiday for the first time. Then things began to go wrong. Dick's plane home broke down on the runway, for the first time in two years. He lost a day while they flew out another aircraft, and then spent a whole night helping to transfer the seats and unloading a replacement engine.

The day before we were to to go on leave, I reported for duty with Ivor. We were greeted by an angry officer and a dismaying question: 'What's all this nonsense about you two going to Austria tomorrow? You can't expect to go touring round the Continent without a passport!' This, after days of checking that an RAF border visa, 'the Key to the Continent', would open every frontier.

While I headed for the monitoring room, Ivor was allowed to dash off and track down the Leave Sergeant, whose misplaced faith in a bit of RAF bumf had left us in limbo. He was unabashed. 'How about Berchtesgaden?' he offered. 'That should be OK. You won't need a passport. It's still in Germany – just. Anyway, it was Hitler's favourite spot.'

The next morning, we were on the platform of Lichtenfelde West station waiting to catch the American Forces train out of Berlin. Already it felt like another country, a little bit of America. Crowds of cropped and gum-chewing American soldiers milled around, bombarded through loudspeakers by American music. A huge American military policeman with a gun told us: 'Show your ID to the Lootenant!' As the train pulled out, the speakers blared 'Auf Wiedersehen' and 'Auld Lang Syne'. I loved America, and all Americans.

We were free at last, rolling through Frankfurt, Heidelberg and Stuttgart to Munich – towns and cities which had existed for me only in wartime news bulletins. Ivor bought a cake, and we carved it up with a nail file. Then we were heading up into mountains, watching the ramparts of the Alps taking shape through the window. I took dozens of hopeless snaps, wasting film in an orgy of release. I thought briefly of that darkened room back in Berlin, and roared through another film.

At the end of a golden afternoon the train came into Berchtesgaden. It was one of those enchanted arrivals you never forget. Maybe it was because we were weary after twenty-four hours of non-stop train travel, but things seemed to unfold with the improbable but inevitable logic of a dream. We met an English-speaking hotel owner on the platform and he led us to his exquisite chalet, perfectly positioned under picture postcard mountains. Sitting in a café, we suddenly saw a couple of guys we'd known at Crail, Naval Linguists on leave from their base at Kiel. In the town square, we enjoyed the comically bad brass band playing oompah music. We climbed a hill to watch an operatic sunset.

The next morning I dashed off a rhapsodic letter to my parents, gushing about 'one of the most breathtaking landscapes I've ever seen'. I was equally impressed with the fixtures in the 'palatial' chalet, 'from bedside lamps to electric razor points'. Just to really give them the flavour of this Bavarian paradise, I actually stuck a strip of the chalet's soft pink toilet paper to the letter. I can only think that the joy of escaping the bounds of Berlin had produced a mild hysteria. 'Our return to captivity feels an eternity away,' I ended.

That whole week glows in my memory, almost half a century later. It's partly the old photos, of course – little square snaps in black and white which record our ecstatic wanderings. There's a shirtless Ivor, rowing us across the huge mirror of the Konigsee, framed in steep mountains. I remember bellowing that this was worth the whole of National Service and hearing the echo bouncing back. There's Ivor grinning over a huge meal in Reith im Winkl. There's me, the romantic traveller gazing enraptured at a snowy mountain. There's Ivor, wandering down a quaint street in Salzburg – our RAF border visas worked after all, and we made it to Austria for a quick trot through Mozart's birth house. There are half a dozen pictures of us with a natty little Volkswagen. Ivor could drive, and pooling our limited cash we hired the car for a day's scamper round the byways along the German/Austrian border, fuelled by grotesque blowout meals.

It all feels achingly innocent now, a polite prelapsarian picnic. In some of the photos, we're even wearing ties. At the time, it felt like a grand compensation for our months in the dark, and somehow for the past two years. For a few days, the Cold War faded.

16

THE LONGED FOR, dreamed of, fantasized about moment was almost here. In my joy, I listed the things I was doing for the last time. My last RAF laundry bundle had just joined the other signposts to freedom. I was relishing the prospect of my final cookhouse queue. I had asked my parents to cancel the weekly postings of *Punch*, the *Listener* and *Melody Maker*.

The accident of joining up a couple of months earlier than anyone else meant that I was going to be the first of my squad of Linguists to break out. Those months back in the autumn of 1956, drudging on the camp rubbish truck and picking up stones at RAF West Malling while I waited for the course to start at Crail, were now paying off. I could exasperate my chums hourly with my relentless countdown and maddening cheeriness.

I spent happy hours scavenging cardboard boxes to send home clothes and books. I started a round of goodbyes. I went into the city for a final shopping trip. Ron tagged along with me on a hunt for a Nazi Iron Cross medal to present as an unlikely competition trophy to his local Scout troop back home. On a cobbled back street, we found an antique shop crammed with hideous paintings of stags and ivory statuettes of Chinese nobles. Ron had his pick of medals in varying states of dilapidation, and finally got his trophy for the equivalent of twenty-five pence. In my demob-happy mood, it felt like a perfect metaphor for the futility of military endeavour.

Of course I still had my duties in the monitoring centre, which seemed to be in a ferment of overwork. Those newcomers had been gobbled up by the scribbling machine but the thing was as insatiable as ever. I was obviously getting out at just the right moment. As my final watch approached, the weary Warrant Officer made what was clearly a heartfelt plea. 'Look, lad, you can see how desperate we are. You can't leave us in the lurch. Why don't you think about signing on for another year?' I couldn't believe he was serious, but I managed to make my excuses without actually laughing out loud.

And then suddenly it was over. I still had no idea what it had all amounted to, those months of cramming Russian in the outbacks of Scotland and Gloucestershire, those interminable hours with the headphones, those thousands of pages of transcribing the routine comings and goings of pilots I knew only by their callsigns. Over the months, I had grown to recognize some of their voices. I sometimes wondered what their lives were like, flying those endless exercises far from home, hoping like us that it would never turn real.

There were many goodbyes to the people I had come to know, some of them colleagues I had lived alongside almost every day for twenty months. I suppose we had spent more hours together than with anyone else thus far in our short lives. We swore that of course we would meet up; we knew we would probably never see one another again. We shook hands with the awkward formality of young men of our time, decades before young men were allowed to hug, the fumbled partings of people who couldn't find any other way to say goodbye. 'Have a good life!' we said.

I hauled my battered kitbag on to a bus and headed out of the camp to retrace my journey back to Britain and home. Before I could make my final escape, I was shunted off to yet another camp at RAF Schafoldendorf for an ultimate security grilling. A stern officer leaned across his desk and stared at me. 'Never forget,' he said, 'that you must never, never tell anyone what you've been doing as a Russian Linguist. This is an order of the greatest importance.' I managed to look solemn.

Then, in a euphoric trance, I passed down the escape tunnel of train and ferry and train again to find myself at a shabby depot not far from Cheltenham. It strikes me now that it must have been close to GCHQ, the hub of the UK's global spy machine. But I had more mundane business. The final act of my life as a spy was to hand back the exhausted remnants of my RAF uniform.

On a perfect afternoon in the early summer of 1958, I stood on a sunny pavement waiting for a bus. I knew with a rush that I had never been as happy in my life. I had the summer ahead of me, I was going to Cambridge, I would learn to drive, I would sleep late, I would see how things stood with the girlfriend. The moment came to a precise focus in the feel of the trousers flapping against my legs – lightweight, civilian trousers. I was free.

PART TWO

GOING BACK

17

'SEE YOU LATER, Alligator.' Sonia, a large woman in a pale blue anorak, enunciated the words carefully. I didn't quite know how to respond. Looking anxious, Sonia added: 'After a while, Crocodile.' Our welcoming party at the airport in Moscow was clearly keen to make us feel at home. Sonia looked up at the leaden sky. 'Soon it will be raining cats and dogs,' she said.

It was June 1986, my first visit to the Soviet Union. In the three decades since my National Service, I had been here many times in my imagination. This part of the world, which President Ronald Reagan had recently dubbed 'The Evil Empire', had become something of a professional and personal obsession. That Soviet version of life, which I had first encountered in East Berlin, had stuck to me. But I had never made it to the place where it all began and ended.

After university, I had got lucky. In June 1961, without much more idea of what it would mean than I'd had when I joined the RAF Linguists, I fumbled my way on to a production trainee course at Granada Television in Manchester. I found I had joined the TV business at a moment when things were taking off. It was the 60s, and new ideas and new technologies were being explored, there was money around for risk-taking, and my bosses at Granada were keen to find new ways of putting the world on television. Best of all for me, the solitary child found a community at last. Granada was to become my home for almost thirty years, stimulating, supporting, shaping who I became. From the beginning, promotion was rapid, and I found myself travelling the world as an itinerant documentary maker by my late twenties.

Someone suggested to me that making documentaries was just another kind of spying. The arrival of new lightweight film technology had transformed our agenda. We could pick up the camera and run with it, we could record sound freed of the tangled umbilical which used to anchor the camera to the tape recorder. And we could embark on investigations – 'gropes', we called them – for the first time. We smuggled the camera into a wardrobe to snoop on a dodgy businessman; we hid the camera in a bag to track down a war criminal; we used hidden cameras and a mike hidden in a fountain pen to film mercenaries running guns into a civil war in Africa; we smuggled cameras to track down torturers in Brazil.

As TV journalism grew bolder, I occasionally recalled our tentative eavesdroppings in Berlin, and reflected how the technology of snooping had blossomed to include even us documentary vagrants. The spooks had their satellites and their orbital surveillance now, we had our Eclaire cameras and Nagra tape recorders, our zoom lenses and our radio mikes. We also had our regrettable safari suits and that high-octane mix of social purpose and mischief which allowed us to think of ourselves – I shudder to admit it now – as rock 'n' roll journalists. Cameramen actually put stickers on their Eclaires, inspired by Pete Seeger's banjo to claim: 'This machine kills fascists!' A *World in Action* colleague recalls finding himself in some late 60s gathering of the righteous, saying: 'George Harrison, I don't believe you've met Robert Mugabe.'

In half a dozen TV films I also tried to get to grips with telling stories about the other side of the Cold War. I had been in Poland and Czechoslovakia and Yugoslavia, always unofficially, on the track of various programmes – spying, I suppose they would have called it. In fact the problems of making films behind the Iron Curtain had compelled me to find a different way of telling my stories. It occurred to me that it was a version of what I had been doing in the monitoring building in another life – listening in and trying to understand. From the information I was able to collect, I had compiled a series of journalistic recreations of events in Eastern Europe. At the beginning of the 80s, I had reconstructed the inside story of the Soviet invasion of Czechoslovakia. I had also recreated the birth of the Solidarity movement in the Gdansk shipyards. Back in 1970, my first tentative dramatized documentary had been a film about events in Russia, a reconstruction of the secret trial of a dissident Soviet army general who was shut away in a mental asylum.

I met the dissident General when he was released in the late 70s, and he told me the KGB had taunted him about my film when he was in prison: 'They said "You have been impersonated by a bourgeois activist."' The General added: 'But I never expected to meet that bourgeois activist!' I rather enjoyed the label, but knowing that the KGB had spotted me didn't encourage me to travel to the heart of my obsession, to Russia and to Moscow.

And now I was here, courtesy, I suppose, of Mr Gorbachev. The astonishing cracking of the Cold War ice which had followed the arrival of a new Soviet leader in 1985 had reached British television. An invitation had been sent to London for a delegation of British TV folk to come and show programmes, and to talk. A dozen of us, drama people, journalists, documentary makers, bosses and programme toilers, had been rounded up for an unprecedented get-together.

The man in the box at Immigration, sallow and suspicious, provided a satisfyingly sinister introduction. He peered doubtfully at my passport photograph. 'Is not you?' I assured him that it was. 'Do you speak Russian?' he asked, looking at me hard. 'Nyet,' I said, before I could stop myself. Paranoia bloomed, sudden and luxuriant. Did they have something in the depths of the KGB about that 'bourgeois activist' and his former life as a spy? But the moment passed and my interrogator waved me on with a weary flap of his hand.

I was through. And it was just as it should be. We rattled towards the city in a taxi which seemed about to expire with every pothole. There were the huge slogans by the roadside, extolling Perestroika in the script I had imbibed so long ago. There were the ranks of workers' flats, and actual heroic workers thronging the pavements, plodding towards a bright new future under Gorby. Sonia pointed out one of the classic Stalinist towers, like a rocket in a Flash Gordon cartoon. 'Highscraper,' she said. It was the Moscow I had always imagined. I was thrilled.

In my shoebox bedroom at the Minsk Hotel on Gorky Street, my excitement was somewhat dented. After running the gauntlet of the dour women in cardigans on reception, I contemplated my doll-scaled wardrobe and bath the size of a bidet. The glimpse of a pretty lime-green church through the ill-fitting curtains was some relief. And I could see no sign of a bugging device in the mouldering light-fitting. But at least another Soviet cliché was gratifyingly confirmed: there were indeed no bath plugs.

Walking into Red Square that night with a couple of fellow TV delegates, I felt my affair with the Cold War adversary who had kept bumping into my life was finally consummated. I was speechless. Nobody had ever told me that the centrepiece of the Evil Empire, the place which had been demonized all my life as the heart of darkness, was gorgeous – and a bit dotty. The pantomime miracle of St Basil's Cathedral, with its mad collection of garish domes, looked like Widow Twankey's fantasy fun palace. The red neon star on the Kremlin towers, the curly battlements of the Kremlin walls, like a vision from the *Arabian Nights*, the blood-coloured ramparts looming over the square – all of it added up to the most magical and overwhelming public space I had ever seen. We stood for a while in front of

Lenin's tomb. Two soldiers goose-stepped up and down with the precision of mechanical toys. I fantasized they could be the sons of that shivering kid I'd met at the Soviet War Memorial in Berlin. Confronted by the red granite bunker which held the remains of the godfather of the Soviet Union, I had a sense of utter familiarity and faint disbelief.

History was still being played out here. This was the precise spot where one side in the Cold War took its stand. I could see the balcony on the roof of Lenin's tomb where the stone-faced Soviet leadership gathered, automata equipped with waving hands, to watch the parades of military might rumble past. Stalin, Khrushchev, Brezhnev had all stood there to survey their tanks and soldiers and missiles. Tonight it was just a couple of British TV folk and a little group of American tourists. But the lights were still on in the offices behind the Kremlin walls, and nobody was sure if this new man Gorby would make a difference.

That first visit to Moscow, scurrying between the maddening mess of the Minsk Hotel and bewildering meetings with Soviet film and television apparatchiks who asked us about our 'art' and our 'class-consciousness', turned the screws even more on my ambiguous affair. The television our hosts wanted to show us was mostly flavourless and dreary, folk-dancing displays, performing dogs doing humiliating things, and conducted tours of monuments. It was almost as drab as the things I'd seen on my bus trip into East Berlin twenty-eight years earlier. But the lovely Russian language swirled round me again, this time not in classrooms or through headphones, but in the streets. Half-forgotten words came back into focus; those Crail teaching dialogues took on characters, and faces. We were welcomed into a tiny cramped apartment for a banquet of 'crushed nuts and hen' and rich Georgian wine, followed by the exchange of songs: 'Kalinka' from our hosts, 'My Bonnie Lies Over the Ocean' from the guests. There was a torrent of toasts about peace and love and friendship. A man from Channel 4 fell over.

Despite the daily absurdities of that first visit – the furious waiters, the dishwater soup, the shops offering nothing but a jar of pickled gherkins, the bum-scouring loo paper – I knew I'd be back. One of our delegation got roughed up by the police for protesting about some kid being excluded from our screening even though he had a ticket. We drove past the looming edifice of the KGB Headquarters, guarded by the statue of its founder, the malign Feliks Dzerzhinsky. I wondered again if my file was locked away there in some fearsome vault. On our final afternoon, we tried to do some shopping in a huge department store near the Bolshoi. Passive queues coiled round the gloomy spaces, waiting in line for hours in the hope of buying a shirt or some plastic shoes. The only neglected stall was selling statuettes of Lenin. It was just one more spectacle of the callous theft of a normal life. Just to look at at that queue made me feel frantic. And hypnotized.

In the Museum of the Revolution I saw a light bulb from the 1920s. The filament at the heart of the bulb was a tiny Lenin. That first visit to Moscow felt like that for me – lit up, and trapped.

I have been back to Russia a dozen times since then. Over those years I was a passing spectator as the huge Communist experiment tottered and fell, like that statue of Dzerzhinsky lassoed round the neck and hauled from his pedestal by ecstatic crowds. In pursuit of TV films, I have made Russian friends in strange places: a Cosmonaut in 'Star City', Russia's shabby space training centre, who played Glenn Miller's 'Moonlight Serenade' in orbit, and another who circuited the earth interminably, trapped in space, as the Soviet Union collapsed below him; a rock 'n' roll writer who dreamed of escaping his country in a hot-air balloon, and was finally given a first-class ticket to London; a Soviet journalist who reported on the rise and fall of Gorbachev and yearned for New York, where he grew up; a Colonel who had commanded Russia's nuclear missile squadrons for twenty years and who told me I was the first foreigner he had ever met. For a graduate of an enemy spy school, the invitation from Russia's 'Rocketchiki' to make a film for Western television in the heart of the country's biggest and most sensitive missile base felt unreal. I decided it was best not to tell the Rocketchiki how I had learned my bit of Russian.

Over those years, as that other world which Winston Churchill had called 'a riddle wrapped in a mystery inside an enigma' became increasingly familiar, I was sometimes asked by Russians where I had picked up something of their language. As the Soviet Union began to recede into history, I felt able to be less evasive about my time as an Air Force Linguist. But as I tried to fit together the bits and pieces of my life as a junior spook all those years ago when I was nineteen and everything was different, I became aware of how little I really knew about what we'd been doing and what it all meant.

After following my Cold War obsession in films for thirty years, I realized I'd never tried to find out how it all started for me. So I did. In my mid-sixties, I discovered an urge to go back down the tunnel of years to explore the forgotten territory where an unworldly teenager was just starting out. I wanted to know what we had been doing with our carbon paper and pencils and whether it had made any difference. I hoped, as well, that the journey might help me to understand something more about my own story.

18

THE PUBLIC Record Office in Kew was a surprise. I did not expect the last resting-place of Britain's old secrets to look like this – a tidy brick complex in the style of a motorway conference centre. A water park in the grounds featured fountains and wading birds as motionless as metal statues. As I approached, one of the birds came to life, swivelling its head to keep a beady eye on me.

I was a few minutes early for my appointment, so I sat on a bench in soft spring sunshine. I became aware that there was a plaque fixed to every seat. They were a roll-call of virtuous resolutions collected from teenagers and installed on the benches by a commercial TV company in a rush of social conscience. To pass the time I started reading some of the inscriptions. 'I will sponsor a child in a third world country.' 'I will recycle and care for the environment of future generations.' 'I will make a difference for people with a learning disability.' Abashed by this parade of noble intentions, it was a relief to come across a couple of less elevated texts: 'I will be an Arsenal fan forever' and 'I will look at

Obi-Wan Kenobi and Darth Maul and live accordingly.'
I wondered what my contribution might have been
when I was a virtuous teenager.

Someone had told me that the Public Record Office,
which sounded like an East German police bunker, used
to be the more sonorous 'National Archive'. Either way,
it seemed a good place to start the hunt for my story.
Along with millions of other bits of yellowing paper, I
gathered that the archive held a score of files detailing
how the Joint Services School for Linguists came into
being, and how it worked. In fact the JSSL material
had only gradually been released in the 1990s after the
collapse of Communism. The final documents hadn't
emerged until 2001.

I was led through hushed corridors into a huge room
where dozens of people crouched at new tables, lost in
old papers. Divided by a maze of glass partitions, the
reading room shifted and reflected the archive hunters
in a fairground hall of mirrors. On my table, a pair of
white cotton gloves were laid out, reprovingly it seemed.
I sat down to wait for the files, trying to assume a due
reverence. An acolyte appeared from some inner sanc-
tum, carrying three bulky files, and laid the offerings in
front of me. Feeling rather foolish, I struggled into the
white gloves.

The drab files were tied up with a string like a
shoelace. Untying the knot and opening the first file,
labelled 'AIR 2/13255', I was instantly hit by the smell
of old documents, stale and musty. My father's hoarded
motoring magazines smelled like that when I found
them in our attic during the war. To me that stink of

old paper was always associated with regret. Maybe it was because the magazines were full of photos of carefree motorists, off on pre-war family jaunts down country lanes to a lost utopia which Hitler had snatched away.

The JSSL files promised a different kind of romance. Behind the anonymous cover, I found a green folder stamped CONFIDENTIAL – AIR MINISTRY. To further repel unauthorized trespassers, the folder was emblazoned with an orange sticker and more warnings: COPY RESTRICTED. It was like entering a top secret weapons store. Adventuring into the folder, I was confronted with a first page stamped SECRET in bright red letters. Flicking through, I saw that every page reminded the impudent reader that this was SECRET too. More recently, some minion with a biro had been through the file drawing a line through each of the red warnings and opening the door to snoopers like me. I wondered what kind of state secrets could have justified all this bureaucratic effort. I dipped into a few pages at random.

Agendas and reports, minutes and memoranda, this was the stuff which had hammered out the shape of JSSL in the 1950s. I looked into one document: 'SUBJECT – Language Training Requirements' – a memo from the 'Language Subcommittee of the OAMC'. The typewritten record summoned up that long-forgotten gathering in Room 133, Adastral House, at 1545 hours. The list of the people present took me back into that room. There were the RAF officers, Group-Captain this and Wing-Commander that; the civil servants with their dusty labels, 'DDM Plans' and 'DDM POL'; and the spooks, hiding behind the anonymity of 'F8' and 'S10c'. I felt

I could almost see them, droning through the long afternoon with their tea going cold, fretting that the smog might come down before they could catch the train home.

The idea of a military school to teach Russian had been born around the time the Soviet Union exploded its first atomic bomb in 1949. Faced with the inescapable reality of Soviet power, in 1950 Prime Minister Clement Attlee urged the creation of a training programme for Russian Linguists. At a time when the Cold War seemed all too likely to turn hot, Britain was deaf to the enemy's intentions. Most Britons regarded learning foreign languages as an outlandish irrelevance. Certainly, it was not a thing a respectable officer would consider. The country had very few Russian speakers, and gathering intelligence behind the Iron Curtain was a hazardous and unreliable business. As the Cold War intensified, it was decided that the armed services needed a crash course to train men, mainly National Servicemen, who could interrogate Russian prisoners, read Russian documents, and listen in on Russian radio communications – which was where I had joined the story.

In the files at the Public Record Office, the muted desperation of bureaucrats trying to juggle the pressures of the Cold War, the penny-pinching of an age of austerity, and the British class system seeped from the pages: 'The serious shortfall in the number of regular officers volunteering to learn a foreign language is causing grave concern. A special sub committee of the Officers and Air Crews Manning Committee has been set up to seek ways of improving the present condition.

Although everything possible will be done to improve the financial inducements, any such inducements will have to be negotiated with the Treasury.'

Still, it appeared that for all the problems, those struggling officials had big plans. The files told of schemes for Linguists to monitor the languages of the world – Romanian, Serbo-Croat, Lithuanian, Arabic, Amharic, Gokali, Kikuyu. Kikuyu? I had a sudden fantasy of a language school in the outer Hebrides where Kenyan tribesmen passed on their wisdom to shivering airmen.

As I explored the other files, I could track the story of JSSL. From its earliest days, in 1950, when the proposal to set up language training was being passed around between academics and intelligence chiefs, a sense of urgency drove the debates. Military chiefs of staff conferred with cabinet ministers. Memos expressed concern that things would not be ready. Draughty Victorian houses in Cambridge and London were purchased. Shabby barrack huts in an army camp near Coulsdon in Surrey were readied; a cheerless camp outside Bodmin in Cornwall, memorable only for its reputation for rain and cold, became the other base for JSSL. In September 1951, the first servicemen began their struggles with the Cyrillic alphabet. Reading the history, I reckoned that I was lucky in being recruited for the Russian Linguists' final gulag in Crail.

Wherever JSSL set up its tent, the course seemed to be much the same. I found a memo which laid out the timetable for the Russian course with a detail which would have satisfied the most fastidious apparatchick in a Stalinist planning ministry. The training, it was decreed, should last for ten months, during which time there should be 880 hours of instruction. The committee estimated that the course would cost £230 per head – a formidable investment in 1950s terms.

Always, there's the worry about money and the challenge of recruiting the raw material for Linguist training. Reading the files, I got the impression that the RAF brass and public school civil servants and spooks manning those committees had much sympathy with the regular service officers who showed little inclination to learn a foreign language. After all, old boy, was the unspoken message, that wasn't the sort of thing a gentleman ought to bother himself with. So, more meetings and more long afternoons were passed in deliberating how to tempt those other ranks, junior technicians and corporals without too much expense. 'After eighteen months' productive service, a Linguist will be made a corporal technician, and paid an extra one shilling and sixpence per day.' I tried to work it out – ten bob, fifty pence per week extra for slogging on in the monitoring centre. Mercifully, I was free long before they would have had to raid the national coffers for my bonus.

So that was it. All these papers stamped 'Secret' and 'Confidential' had been hoarded for fifty years 'to protect national security'. For a dozen years after the collapse of the old Cold War enemy, the dry administrative details of pay-scales for Linguists in the 1950s, the minutes of those hundreds of meetings, the budgets and the timetables for setting up JSSL had been deemed too sensitive to see the light of day. As I began my search, those dusty non-secrets in the files at the Public Record Office felt like a perfect metaphor for the paranoid delusions of the espionage trade.

19

I WENT BACK TO Scotland to look for my old spy school. On a pretty morning in late March, the road from Edinburgh along the Fife coast was disarmingly likeable. Could this really be the route I travelled on those panicky Monday morning dashes back to camp after weekends at home? The little towns with their comic names – Pittenweem, Largo – still had their dispiriting enclaves of pebble-dashed council houses; but the constant presence of the sea behind green fields gave my drive a holiday feel.

Just beyond Anstruther, I got a surprise. On a back road I saw a sign for 'The Secret Bunker'. Surely the wooden huts where I learned Russian hadn't become a high-tech James Bond command centre. A few yards further, I got my answer. A hoarding invited me to visit 'Scotland's Best Kept Secret. Discover the twilight world of the Cold War. Take the opportunity to discover how the Government would have survived, and you wouldn't!!!' The thing had been there since the early 1950s, and must have been brooding away under the Fife fields when I was gearing up my Russian just

down the road in Crail. The hoarding said the entrance
to the bunker had been concealed under an innocent-
looking farmhouse, and no hint of our VIP neighbour
had ever reached us. Now, the top persons' nuclear
bunker had become a tourists' theme park.

I drove up to the gate, but everything looked shut. A
cheerful woman with a carrier bag came out of a door.
'I'm afraid we're closed until April,' she said, 'but you
should definitely come back. It's really interesting.' A
rusting missile launcher crouched in the car park.
Dramatic posters gushed on about '3 ton blast proof
doors' . . . '100 feet below the earth' . . . 'the tensest
moments of the Cold War'. I doubted whether the
excitements of visiting an old air-raid shelter would
seduce me to trek back to the edge of Scotland. Still,
I was intrigued. Clearly the locals could be relied on to
keep their mouths shut. But was there something in the
air of this quiet Fife backwater which nurtured secrets?

Driving down the single main street of Crail banished
any potential for paranoia. The sober little town which
had been my home ground in another life was transformed. Cute galleries and gift shops nuzzled up against
the 'Heritage Centre'. A man on a ladder was sprucing
up the paintwork on an old house. I spotted a mobile
sculpture in a cottage window. The dour citizens of
Crail would have had no truck with all this frippery in
my time. I saw a sign pointing up the road which used
to lead to JSSL. It said 'The Crail Raceway'.

SO HERE I WAS AGAIN, forty-seven years after I first
rattled down that road, looking for the place where it all

began. I felt something of that first flutter of anticipation about what I might find. It was utterly familiar, the road ruled straight between fields, sea just as I remembered, lining the horizon on the right. But would there still be any trace of the old camp? Would it be buried under a housing estate or collapsed into rubble?

Suddenly, it was there. The grey huts huddled on a hillside behind rusting barbed-wire fences had the feel of an old film I half recalled. I almost expected to see distant figures in uniform, but there were only bored-looking sheep. I pulled up alongside a sign which told me this was now 'May Rock Industrial Estate' and 'David Robertson Farms Ltd'. But what I was looking at was the little building where our fates were posted on a noticeboard long ago. The board was gone, the building was a roofless shell. A tractor loaded with turnips rattled by.

I walked into the camp. It was a glorious morning now. The buildings in front of me were the ghosts of the teaching blocks where we were drilled in Russian. The shape of the place was still somehow imprinted in me. If I turned left here, I should find my classroom. And here it was. The building looked like a casualty of war. Every window was smashed, doors leaned off their hinges. Turnips were piled against the end wall like a snowdrift.

I went through a door, crunching on rubble and broken glass. Peering into a room carpeted with old bricks, a bush sprouting in the corner, I had a flash of memory. I'm sitting here in my thick RAF uniform, still damp from the drizzle outside. There are a dozen of us, slumped at shabby desks listening to a tired-looking man. A chart behind him lists the Russian alphabet. With weary patience, the instructor enunciates for the tenth time some nuance of pronunciation.

The sound of a broken window frame banging in the wind pulled me back. I saw that the hut was stripped clean of the smallest hint that JSSL and its Linguists had ever passed this way. It was almost as though someone had been there and wiped away the evidence, like a criminal cleaning up the scene of his crime. I wandered the corridors and decaying rooms, trying to find something to make my memories real. Finally, in a small side room I found a clue. Half a dozen rusty coat hooks were still jutting from a wall. They would have to serve as some kind of memorial.

Outside again, I tried to get my bearings. As I looked around for something familiar, a shiny black four-wheel-drive pulled up alongside me. A beefy man in a pink shirt surveyed the interloper with obvious suspicion. 'Can I help you?' he said. Before I could explain myself, he added, 'You're not from "Historic Scotland"?' Clearly this was not a good thing to be as far as the man in the pink shirt was concerned. He made it sound as though 'Historic Scotland' might be a Celtic offshoot of al-Qaeda. I was happy to set him straight, and he visibly relaxed. He introduced himself as Will Robertson. 'I'm the owner here,' he said. I gushed out a potted account of why I was nosing around his property – National Service, JSSL, a trip down Memory Lane. He invited me to come to his office for a chat and drove off.

Robertson had said his office was located in what I had known as the camp cinema and gymnasium. The building, a pebble-dashed barn of a place, looked just as I remembered it. I pushed through a door into the lobby and found the little box office was still waiting for the customers who would never return. A stopped clock leaned on the counter. Through another door and I was in the gymnasium, for some reason scattered with old Pepsi dispensing machines. But that wasn't all. Like a jolt from a horror movie, I suddenly saw the rope. Dangling from the ceiling was the instrument of my youthful torments. This had to be the very rope I had struggled to climb, urged on by a heartless sergeant. Why should this, of all relics, remain as a grizzly memento of my time at JSSL? Memory Lane had suddenly darkened. I backed away and stumbled out of the building.

Will Robertson's office was tucked away on top of the cinema, a refuge from the dank crypt below. Robertson sat at his desk under a picture of a racing car and told me his troubles. 'Historic Scotland has scheduled the site as an Ancient Monument, which is basically limiting anything we want to do here.' Years of presiding over the mouldering remains of my old spy school and doing battle with Historic Scotland seemed to have bound him to the place. 'They class it like a Roman Fort,' he said, with the weary chuckle of a man who has fought a long and taxing campaign.

Robertson pulled out a letter and began to read it to me. It was from the fearsome Inspector at Historic Scotland. 'As I think you will appreciate, concern for the conservation of military structures dating from the two world wars is a fairly recent development.' I felt I could almost hear the scratch of a quill pen in the Inspector's office. 'Within Historic Scotland, we feel it is very important that we should now give very careful attention to the needs and potential of such sites as a whole.' Maintaining what I thought was an impressively neutral tone, Robertson ploughed into a lengthy proposal for a 'meeting to explore a mutually acceptable way forward' and the 'need to find funding for an independent feasibility study'. He put the letter down. 'That was four years ago,' he said, 'and we're still in limbo. If they delay much longer, the roofs will fall in.'

Meanwhile, JSSL had become a pig farm. Robertson told me the billets where Linguists had lived and crammed were now accommodation for his herd of porkers. Leaning back in his chair, he said, 'There's none of the atmosphere of what they call a military fortification – apart from the grunt of pigs.'

For all the frustrations of his long tussle with the guardians of Scottish history, Robertson had found a way to breathe some life into his Cold War fossil. 'We've diversified from agriculture to tourism and motor sports,' he told me. 'There's a booming market in track days.' The camp's old airstrip, a relic of its days as a torpedo training base, was now a Mecca for car nuts. Liberated by the five-mile runway, tearaways from far and wide relished the chance to hurl their souped-up hot rods at the horizon, insulated from the attentions of the Crail constabulary. 'We get eight thousand spectators some weekends,' Robertson said. 'Unfortunately the only way to get here is via Crail mainstreet.' I sensed the locals might not be entirely happy.

Then there were the movies. Improbably, Hollywood had found its way to Fife and Will Robertson's folly had given a home to a succession of films and TV dramas. The isolation of the place and those miles of old airstrip had allowed the fantasy merchants to indulge their production designers and special effects crackpots to the full. Robertson talked dreamily of the time when a film company flooded the runway with wax to simulate an ice-filled harbour.

Robertson had told me that the upper camp where the pigs had now moved into our old dormitories was under foot and mouth restrictions. I could go up for a sentimental look, as long as I didn't get out of the car. 'Oh, and by the way,' he said, 'the place you remember as the parade ground is now our manure heap.'

I parked alongside a row of barrack huts, trying to focus my memory. Sheep nibbled the grass where we had lined up for a group photo. I cruised past pig pens and found what I thought was my hut. There was a new yellow sign on the door, warning: 'DANGER! FRAGILE ROOF.' Two giant pigs peered at me. I moved on to tour the dung heap. It sat the middle of the parade ground where we had assembled every morning before marching off for another day of Russian cramming. It was all very soothing, I thought. Mouldering huts, grazing sheep, snuffling pigs, dung. There was something satisfying about this spectacle of rural decay, and the way those years of Cold War striving were being rubbed out in a quiet pastoral invasion.

Suddenly the idyll was blasted to bits by two jet fighters screaming low over the camp from the nearby base at RAF Leuchars. Time to go. As a sea fog rolled in, I bumped away down the hill and headed into Crail. I had a hankering to try to excavate the Music Box Café, and my first encounter with Elvis and that jukebox.

The main street was mysterious now, the fog smudging the solid stone buildings. I walked past houses and a couple of shops looking for something familiar, but the Music Box seemed to have vanished. I went into the post office, but the chatty woman behind the counter was too young to remember my Crail. I asked in a gift shop, but the best they could do was to offer me a place mat printed with the crest of HMS *Jackdaw*, the torpedo training centre which had preceded JSSL in the camp down the road. 'You might try the carpet shop,' the assistant suggested. 'Maybe the old man over there would remember something.'

From somewhere behind the rolls of carpet in the back of the shop, they summoned a sprightly pensioner. 'Aye,' he said, 'that would have been yon place next door. It's just a house these days.' Outside again, though it looked impossible, I knew he was right. The tiny bungalow shut away behind net curtains was as dour as a manse. It was hard to match it up with my memories of the gurgling coffee machine and the jukebox and Elvis. An elderly woman with a shopping bag stared at me disapprovingly and went into the house mumbling something. It sounded like a curse.

In the Crail Heritage Centre, I found a little display about JSSL. I looked at the remnants of our time here –

a few photos, a teaching book, a couple of copies of the JSSL magazine *Samovar*, a JSSL tie. The woman who ran the centre had fond memories of jolly dances at the camp. She didn't think much of the old place now. 'It's just an eyesore,' she said. 'And the crowds who come for those car races on the airfield make it almost impossible to get across the street at weekends.'

I headed down the road to St Andrews. In the Westport Bar, a doleful Australian with a stud in his nose whinged about the posh students who slurped five-pound Martinis. In a corner, an American girl yelled gossip at her friend. I had a flash of memory – my nineteen-year-old self, decked out in cavalry twill trousers, blazer and pakamac, daring a St Andrews teashop. At least, I thought, the Bottle Dungeon will still look like the Bottle Dungeon. It had kept its dismal integrity for 500 years when I made my regular pilgrimages in the 1950s. But maybe it had become an internet café or a wine bar?

The entrance to St Andrews Castle was not encouraging. Under a glass canopy reminiscent of a posh garden centre, a daunting range of heritage items were on sale. Tartan gewgaws jostled with statuettes of Highland cattle. A man with a head like Lenin and tartan trousers was standing at the cash desk. 'Do you still do visits to the Bottle Dungeon?' I asked him. 'Of course,' he replied. It didn't sound as though the hellhole had been tarted up with Laura Ashley wallpaper after all. I followed the tartan trousers down the ancient stone steps and into the crypt.

Thrillingly, it was all just the way I remembered. In

keeping with the current requirement for a 'dungeon experience', there was perhaps rather more personal input than I recalled from the austere guide of my youth. Tartan Trousers told me: 'The lucky ones were the ones that got a wee shove down into the dungeon because they would die fairly rapidly.' There was also a vivid new story, worthy of Tarantino, about 'Cardinal Beaton, Archbishop of St Andrews, who was murdered in 1547 and preserved in a box of salt stored in the Bottle Dungeon'. But reassuringly, George Wishart still burrrned at the stake just as as he had in my time.

The guide clattered away up the stairs to welcome a new tour group, leaving me with the dungeon. I looked down into the pit. What was that stuff shining down there in the gloom? It was money. So it seemed that some visitors saw the ghastly pit as a wishing-well these days. Three coins in the dungeon? There was probably some kind of message in all that, but I couldn't work out what it might be.

20

PUCKLECHURCH WAS ELUSIVE. On a perfect spring
morning, I cruised the lovely slopes of south Gloucestershire scanning the signposts – Yatton Keynell, West
Littleton, Fishponds – quiet villages off the beaten track
even now, almost half a century after I was last here. I
was only a few miles south of the M4, but the teeming
artery to the west from London was as unimaginable
now in these folded valleys as it was in the 1950s before
the motorways came.

At last I saw a sign for the place where my old spys'
finishing school had been located. Down a wooded hill
and I was in Pucklechurch – and then out of it again,
without a hint of anything I recognized. I turned round
in a lane tunnelling between overhanging trees and
drove back to the village centre. But the classic English
cluster of old houses and sleepy village shops round a
thirteenth-century church stirred no memories for me
of my own history in these parts. I asked a woman
pushing a pram if she knew anything about an old
RAF camp round here. She looked blank and then said
I might try the trading estate on the edge of the village.

PUCKLECHURCH TRADING CENTRE announced itself in shining chromium letters on an immaculate wall. This had to be it, but I was still struggling to recognize anything. A substantial red-brick building was set in high walls topped by scary-looking razor wire. I parked and went for a closer look. A smart sign declared 'Premier Prison Services – committed to racial equality'. In a cubicle, a few guards in blue uniforms were chatting. I got the attention of a smiling woman and gave her my routine patter about how I was there doing National Service when dinosaurs roamed the earth. 'Can I have a look round?' I concluded. 'I'm afraid you'll have to write to the Home Office,' said the woman warder pleasantly.

I went outside again and came across another notice. Headed 'Mission Statement', this one said: 'We will treat young people as individuals, recognizing that they have different needs and are capable of change.' Yet another plaque proclaimed: 'Vision Statement – We will provide young people with opportunities for self improvement.' So this was what had become of the place where I had struggled to untangle Russian military chatter from Wimbledon commentaries. In an even more Orwellian transformation, the World War II Barrage Balloon centre was now a Young Offenders' Prison, walled in behind a fortress of politically correct slogans. I wondered how the young offenders behind the wall, toiling away at their self-improvement, would feel if they knew what we Linguists had been doing during our spell of incarceration in Pucklechurch. I didn't recall our instructors devoting attention to our 'different needs'. The youngsters might decide they had the better deal, I thought.

But I still hadn't managed to track down any evidence of my time here. I went round the back of the Martian prison, and at last I saw something familiar. Behind a security fence, tucked in alongside anonymous warehouses, I could see a scatter of wooden huts. The man on the gate had an earring and appeared friendly. When I'd given him my potted version of what I did in the Cold War, he said, 'No problem – have a look round.'

The forlorn wooden huts were painted grey now, huddled together like refugees in a strange land. I peered through a grimy window. Nothing – just a bare empty room. This was the place where I had been force-fed military Russian, plugged into headphones for days on end. But it was even harder than at Crail to recover the way it had been. A man trundled a lawnmower, insistent as a buzz saw, over a patch of grass. An articulated truck the size of a house roared out of a warehouse on its way to deliver the stuff which was now the business of my old spy crammer: concrete, frozen food, polystyrene. A notice on the side of an old hut said 'SCRAP'.

Then, sellotaped to a window, I spotted an official-looking piece of paper. Headed 'Temporary Preservation Order', the form stated that the huts were being assessed as 'historic remains' – but only for six months. It seemed I was just in time to catch a final hint of RAF Pucklechurch before the trading estate gobbled up the last crumbs.

This was hardly a place to stir sentimental memories for me. It would take a John Betjeman to excavate any hint of suburban poetry from such an unlovely spot; and the inevitable triumph of one more industrial estate was dispiriting. I suppose even polystyrene is better than Cold War paranoia. Still, the razor wire on the feature-less wall of the PC prison which enclosed my old camp defined a landscape resolutely drained of everything on behalf of trade and vision statements.

I wanted to try to find the place where I had signed the Official Secrets Act. I wandered into one of the old World War II balloon hangars. Cavernous as a cathedral, it was entirely empty, stripped of any hint of its old story. Not even the frozen-food merchants had found any use for this leftover relic. It was time to be gone. Storm clouds as bulky as those barrage balloons hung over the prison wall as I drove away. The gate-keeper with the earring waved goodbye.

Half an hour up the M5 in a service station, a sudden rainstorm hammered on the car roof. I dug out a brochure I had been sent by Bob McNally, PR for Britain's spying centre, GCHQ in Cheltenham. The spooks were reputed to be embracing a new Glasnost, opening the door to the public for the first time. So far, the evidence seemed pretty modest. There had been an exhibition in Cheltenham on the theme of spying through the ages, featuring a fifth-century secret scroll from the war between Greeks and Persians. But the challenge of orchestrating public relations for a highly secret enterprise seemed to be getting to McNally. 'You're causing me some concerns,' he had told me on the phone when I asked if he had any photos of the exterior of GCHQ. I suggested that Tony Blair's intel-ligence torments were perhaps a bigger worry at a moment when British troops were hunting for those elusive weapons of mass destruction in Iraq. Still, at least I had the brochure.

Entitled 'How GCHQ came to Cheltenham', it was fastidiously historical, released for the fiftieth anniversary of the spooks' arrival in the town in 1953 after quitting their old bunker in Bletchley Park. GCHQ, Government Communications Headquarters, had been the ultimate destination for all my scribblings in Berlin. It was the place where the tributaries of intelligence from all over the world flooded in to be analysed, and I recalled that several JSSL people had served time there. Now I wanted to take a look at it.

The rain had turned the motorway into an uninviting river, so while I waited for the storm to subside, I munched a Mars bar and looked at the GCHQ brochure. It was full of good news. 'How fortunate they were to be members of a department which, through a combination of good luck and careful planning, had made its home in a beautiful town in a magnificent countryside.' There were glowing references to drama and choral groups, to chess and hockey and cricket teams. I gathered the GCHQ soccer team had won the Civil Service Cup. Spooks in boots sounded a bit like a Monty Python sketch.

The place wasn't hard to locate. Signposts led me like a flarepath laid out for a plane touching down to land an agent in occupied France. On a suburban ring road, there it was. It looked more like a building site for a new Tesco than a James Bond fantasy. I had seen a TV news item about a scheme for a refurbished GCHQ, so I had some idea of what was going on. The spooks had commissioned an £800-million marvel, 'a super secret space age project', as the breathless reporter put it. Clearly, spying was booming in the twenty-first century. An artist had dreamed up a vision of how it would be. On TV it looked like a set for *Star Wars*, a glowing citadel of concentric galleries and impenetrable code vaults. There was to be an underground computer centre big enough to hold St Paul's Cathedral. There would be a street a third of a mile long with shops and cafés and restaurants. It sounded like an espionage utopia.

Viewed now through my rain-spattered window, the magic drained away in a muddy wasteland. Police cars roamed by. I recalled that the TV report had mentioned that the new GCHQ was designed to resist terrorist mortar attacks. It was obvious that the intelligence-gathering business in the age of terror was as far removed from my scribblings in Berlin as this espionage citadel was from those wooden huts on the edge of Scotland. Surveillance cameras gazed at me from every direction as I drove up to a temporary gate. I had heard that Britons now have more cameras watching over us than in any other place on earth – 4½ million robot spies. Facing this vast apparatus of sleuthing and spookery, it was all too easy to slip into an Orwellian paranoia. It felt as though that British talent for espionage was coming home to haunt us.

A man in a Day-Glo jacket waved me away. It began to rain again, and I headed for home. All along the motorway, the speed cameras kept watch over me.

21

AT THE GHOST OF Checkpoint Charlie, the Albanian souvenir hustlers dragged plastic sheets over their bits of Berlin Wall to protect them from a sudden snow flurry. The tourists abandoned their posing and picture-taking in front of the imitation US Army Guard hut. Just yards from the spot where a young man had been gunned down by East German border guards, visitors dived into the Checkpoint Charlie Museum to buy their Berlin Wall key rings and bars of Berlin Wall chocolate. With the remnants of the real wall shipped off to museums in America and Japan, the Cold War themepark looked more tatty than ever.

I went back to Berlin to try and excavate my time there, when the world was another place. The city which had seen more than its share of the twentieth century's craziness had a convalescent feel, I thought. In the decades since I'd first arrived on the front line of the Cold War, the Wall had come and gone, taking with it the vast Communist experiment.

Over my years as a documentary nomad, I have dipped into a catalogue of the towns and cities refashioned by

Communism: Moscow, Warsaw, Budapest, Beijing, all somehow scarred by the great idea. The ghastly concrete fantasies of People's Moscow or the scary blocks of workers' flats in Poznan – 'fit for heroes of labour' – cling to my memory like the polluting smog which so often seemed to surround them. I found the towns on the edge of the map even more numbing – Gagarin, a forgotten slum of a place where the pioneer astronaut grew up; Szczecin, where Polish shipworkers were gunned down by their leaders; a commune workshop outside Shanghai where workers toiled in hourly danger of amputation; Tatischevo on the Volga, where Russia's élite ballistic missile squadrons are based alongside a village of medieval squalor – all of them, it seemed to me, bore the imprint of rulers who had long ago been poisoned in the decay of an ideology.

Berlin was the start of it for me, and of course the city had its own special drama. Returning to Berlin in the 1980s, I found the Wall had warped and redefined the city I had known. The Brandenburg Gate was shut away now, peering over the top of the Wall like a prisoner glimpsed at a cell window. Remembered streets ended in blind alleys, tram tracks ran into dead ends. By then of course, the Berlin Wall was more than twenty years old, and it seemed it would last for ever, an ugly scar as permanent as the Great Wall of China.

I looked around the little museum next to the Wall at Checkpoint Charlie. The sad collection of objects and photographs charted the awful years since I'd been in Berlin. It was a story of the desperation driving hundreds of attempts to escape. A tinny little Trabant car with a secret compartment where a girlfriend was hidden, a hot-air balloon which drifted a whole family over the Wall, a glider made from the cardboard centres of toilet rolls. The museum recounted desperate tales of escapes inside spare tyres, a rock band's loudspeakers, a submarine made from barrels. Over the years, 5,000 people had made it through the Wall. More than 100 had died.

I had to pass through the Wall for a few hours in 1987 and the experience stays with me as an absurdist black comedy. As a first act, I had to run the gauntlet of Checkpoint Charlie, one of the few arteries still connecting West and East Berlin. It was an artery blocked by the garbage of Cold War paranoia: watchtowers, the 'death strip', barriers rising and falling like guillotines to chop off any hint of normal human contact. An East German guard peered out at me through a little hatch, a sceptical priest ready to hear my sins, his pale face illuminated by white neon. Another 'defender of Socialism' pushed a wheeled mirror under my car. Everything happened in slow motion. Finally I was admitted to the other world on the far side of the Wall, the German Democratic Republic. Instantly, I was back in 1958 and that bus tour almost twenty years earlier.

The rubble of war was gone, but the city sealed up behind Checkpoint Charlie seemed frozen in time. I was trying to track down an LP for a film, and I spotted a record shop on the Alexanderplatz. I joined a stoical queue on the cold pavement outside the door. A dirty orange curtain was pushed aside and a customer came out. One of the queue was allowed into the shop, and the curtain closed again. After a fifteen-minute wait, it was my turn. The record shop had the hush of a funeral parlour. A matron in a blue uniform instructed me to pick up a small orange basket. Apparently any records purchased were required to be carried to the cashier in the basket. I found my record. It wouldn't fit in the basket. None of the records in the shop would fit in the baskets. The matron in blue watched my fumblings impassively. I had a momentary flashback of my parents' record shop in Halifax and my mother watching over her wooden boxes full of 78s. Her shop had a flickering fluorescent light too. I fled.

At the end of a long day, I drove back towards Checkpoint Charlie. It was dark, and I was weary of negotiating the edicts of petty officials and watching my rear-view mirror for suspicious cops. Almost at the Checkpoint, I realized I had a problem. Like every visitor to the East, I had been obliged to change some Western money into East German Ostmarks. Since there had been virtually nothing to buy, I still had bundles of the useless stuff in my pocket. But I knew those guards at Checkpoint Charlie wouldn't let me take it out through the Wall. I turned the car round. Near the old Reichstag building I spotted the only solution. I spilled the worthless notes into a rubbish bin. I felt light-headed with the lunacy of my day in the Communist wonderland. I found myself proclaiming out loud: 'It's all shit, all of it, from here to Vladivostok!' A police car cruised into view, and I scuttled back towards the glow in the sky, the decadent neon excess of my world.

Now the Wall was gone, the absence of the thing felt like an amputation. It had given the huge city a shape, deformed but horribly glamorous. The vast spaces of Potsdamerplatz where the Wall had sliced the world in two were filled with towering consumer cathedrals – multiplexes and computer stores and video screens. Corridors led to more corridors, escalators slithered in empty hallways, a robotic voice in a glass-walled lift intoned the passing levels.

I was coming back to a city where one in three people had arrived in the past ten years. The sudden trauma of German reunification had left Berlin with more than 100,000 empty houses, and new Berliners were flooding in. Turkish gay bars and Arabic restaurants were bringing a new buzz to districts which had mouldered behind the Wall for thirty years. 'Too many Muslims in Berlin,' was the view of the old curmudgeon I talked to in a car park. But he was, it seemed, an equal opportunity racist. When I asked him where he'd learned his English, he told me he'd been a prisoner of war in a camp near Glasgow. 'Scotsmen good, English . . .' He stuck his finger under his nose and pushed it up. Stuck up or smelly, I was clearly an unwelcome visitor to one Berliner.

At the Brandenburg Gate, lost during my time behind a tangle of weeds and barbed wire, I watched hundreds of runners in the Berlin Marathon, brightly attired, pattering through the archways. Their running shoes made a noise like flapping birds. Nearby, a sinister smiling man in a bowler hat and a suit like an undertaker worked the handle of a barrel organ, pumping out jolly music. He could have been an extra left over from *The Third Man*.

Leading away from the Brandenburg Gate, Unter den Linden had been Berlin's stylish mainstreet in the Nazi years. Immaculate officers and well-dressed women had relaxed in cafés and restaurants and in the glamorous Adlon Hotel. This was the Germany of those unmentionable snapshots my father had brought back from his band tour in the 30s, the photos where swastikas fluttered on big flags over the street. The apparatus of Hitler's state machine had run the Third Reich from the nearby streets.

I had seen a newsreel item about Berlin in the days just after World War II. A numbing sequence filmed from the air with the camera moving for minutes on end over the Brandenburg Gate and down Unter den Linden revealed a wasteland of ruins. On the ground, we were shown lines of women, passing stones from hand to hand in a seemingly hopeless attempt to clear the rubble that had been their city. On my brief trip down Unter den Linden and into the Soviet sector a dozen years after the war, the street was still a shellpocked casualty of war. Only the forbidding Soviet Embassy, which looked out on its client state from a commanding position just behind the Brandenburg Gate, seemed to have been fully restored.

Now the blue and white Russian flag fluttered in a chilly wind over the Embassy. Unter den Linden was once again a prosperous artery of the new Germany, lined with forbiddingly opulent car showrooms and chic restaurants. The shiny Mercedes were rolling up again in front of the rebuilt Adlon Hotel.

But I gathered that not everyone was entranced by

the spectacle of the new Berlin. On my hotel TV I watched an episode of *Die DDR Show* and wondered if it could be for real. The gorgeous East German ice skater Katerina Witt flitted down a staircase in her Communist Young Pioneer's uniform – remodelled of course to emphasize the best bits of Katerina – to host a programme full of yearning for the vanished East Germany. It seemed as improbable as me going on television to regret the passing of food rationing and pudding-basin haircuts in 50s Britain. Posed in front of awful mementos of Commy kitsch, a sequence of witnesses lamented the passing of state-produced gherkins and dismaying frocks and cardboard Trabant cars and toxic fruit drinks. Even the old East Berlin street crossing signs were cult objects now. 'The Ampelmann' in his perky little trilby who used to tell obedient Socialist citizens when to cross the road was being recycled as bumper stickers and badges and fridge magnets. 'Ostalgie', nostalgia for life on the wrong side of the Berlin Wall, was, it seemed, in full swing. I wondered whether there might not be some clues in all this for my own ambiguous obsession with life behind the Wall, and the connections with my own isolated growing-up as a child of austerity. But I couldn't discover any yearning to dress up in a belted raincoat or to reconstruct the agonies of a youth club dance.

BEFORE I HEADED OFF to look for my old Berlin spy base I felt I needed a dose of reality. Between the glitter of the Potsdamerplatz and the bruised fantasies of Ostalgie, I wanted to remind myself of how things had been when I was here and the Cold War shaped the world. I drove out past the longest surviving stretch of Berlin Wall, bordering the River Spree. More than a decade after it had lost its meaning, it was still a sobering spectacle. Spooling past me like a film strip, the unbroken sequence of pictures and messages etched on to the brutal concrete by generations of protesters trapped behind the Wall had the awful power of graffiti in the cell of a condemned prisoner: 'No more Walls, no more Wars' . . . 'Get human' . . . 'Do it!' . . . 'Total Democracy'. There were interspersed cartoons and portraits of Elvis, Kennedy, Adam and Eve. In one hideous image, the East German leader Erich Honecker was deep-kissing Leonid Brezhnev. Some of the murals were clearly recent, but further along the paint was peeling and faded, so that the thing felt organic, still alive somehow, with a power to control and restrain.

A couple of miles further, I found the place I was looking for. The former headquarters of East German State Security, the Stasi, is a huge gloomy citadel ranged around a bleak courtyard. When I was scribbling away in the monitoring room at RAF Gatow and for thirty years afterwards, this place was the heart of one of the world's most remorseless surveillance tyrannies. With a determination that would have impressed the Gestapo, 85,000 full-time officers kept watch over their fellow citizens. Another 150,000 people were paid to inform on family, friends and neighbours. Letters were opened, phones were tapped and taped, homes and offices and bars were bugged. The angle of domestic TV aerials was calibrated to catch disloyal viewers of Western television.

Two-thirds of church leaders were recruited as inform-
ers. Under the Stasi spying became a gigantic national
paranoia, a grotesque nightmare ceaselessly feeding on
its own suspicions. In return for their obedience, East
Germans were absolved by the regime from any res-
ponsibilty for the Nazi era. All that, they were told,
happened on the other side of the Wall.

For years, I had wanted to see the Stasi citadel. In
the depths of the Cold War, it was inevitably one of
the most secret and impenetrable bastions on earth. A
copper-lined room shielded Stasi meetings from satellite
surveillance. When the Wall came down, Stasi officers
embarked on an orgy of shredding, frantic to destroy
the evidence of their labours. They were faced with more
than 100 miles of records. When furious citizens ram-
paged through the Stasi HQ, tearing open files and
hunting for evidence of how they had been betrayed,
they found scores of exhausted shredding machines.
The Stasi had fled, but their desperate efforts to wipe
out the evidence of their forty years of tyranny had been
interrupted. Terrible stories were revealed about the
treacheries of friends and the denunciations of work-
mates. And now, as is the way of things these days, the
ultimate source of all this horror has become a quiet
museum.

I wandered through the rooms, alone except for the
distant voice of a tour guide reciting a litany of enormi-
ties for a couple of bored-looking visitors. Arrayed in a
succession of glass cases, the machinery of snooping
seemed almost comic. The camera hidden in a watering-
can, the hymnbook with a concealed microphone, the

car door with an embedded infra-red device, were loony enough. Even my wildest schoolboy spy fantasies could never have come up with this stuff. A shrine with a bust of Lenin and an oil painting of a barrel-chested man laden with medals celebrated Erich Mielke, the Stasi supremo for more than thirty years. He began his rule, I noted, just as I was arriving to begin my own humbler sleuthing career in Berlin. Mielke's office was also on display, frozen in an inhuman tidiness. Chairs stood on parade facing polished tables, telephones were arranged in formation. Wooden walls loomed over wooden floors under a wooden ceiling. It felt like a coffin. It was a style I had last come upon in the KGB Headquarters in Moscow, where a maze of windowless corridors locked in the hermetic fantasies of the spymasters.

The Stasi bunker had other, more disturbing memorials to a state drunk on fear. A shoe with a dagger in the toe made a hideous reality of James Bond's fiendish adversary, Rosa Kleb. I peered at a pair of jars, pondering their mad purpose. It was worse than I could have imagined. The catalogue informed me that these were the containers in which the Stasi had stored the smells of subversives, often harvested from their stolen underwear. Primed with the scents, Stasi killer dogs with their vocal cords removed to conceal their approach could do their work.

22

I DROVE WEST through the city, looking for Gatow. As I left the centre, things were suddenly familiar. Here was the nondescript box which I remember as the NAAFI club, where I first saw the news of Sputnik. It still had the strange tangle of metal struts on its roof, like some remnant of a rocket attack. Now the place had become a computer store and 'the new Berlin Cabaret Club'.

Following the tram tracks into the western suburbs, I replayed the memory of those journeys long ago when I rattled in and out of the city, crammed in alongside suspicious locals. Here was the remembered sign for the Olympic Stadium, and the place where I used to change trams. There were supermarkets now, and aerobic centres by the roadside, but I felt I could still have found my way on autopilot. When I came to the turn for Gatow, it seemed inevitable.

It was prosperous out here, neat restaurants and tidy villas interspersed with a succession of health centres and sanatoriums. Up a rise and a mile or so further, I was at the gateway of my old spy centre, RAF Gatow.

It was a bit of a shock. Painted a garish orange yellow, the archway announced that this was now 'General Steinhof Kaserne'. I had heard that the base had reverted to its original Luftwaffe owners, but the startling paint job was more reminiscent of the *Big Brother* house than a military base. More unsettling still, there were signs for the 'Gatow Golf Club'. I knew that the new Germany was resolutely unmartial, but surely they hadn't handed over their air force to men armed with trolleys and golf clubs?

I attempted a conversation with the private security man at the gate, but we were stranded by our comprehensive lack of a common language. For the hundredth time, I lamented my failure to learn some kind of German during those long months when I was stationed here. Defeated by my babblings about how I'd used to be here, the security man disappeared to make a phone call. A few minutes later, a moustached giant in a green uniform appeared. I noted he had a gun on his belt, but he had enough English to encourage me to embark on a brief account of my time here almost fifty years ago. I thought it was probably best not to complicate things with talk about spying, and I asked if I could come in and have a look round. The giant looked puzzled, but he didn't, as I had feared, summon the military police. This was, after all, a moment when Germany's British and American allies were raining bombs on Iraq, and the world was on high alert. Germany's refusal to get involved might be infuriating George Bush, but it appeared to be making the guardians of General Steinhof Kaserne more relaxed about my trip down Memory Lane.

I followed the green giant's Vauxhall Astra into a half-remembered dreamscape. The road through the pine forest and into the camp had been rearranged, blurred by a bewildering displacement of buildings and greenery. This was the road I had tottered along, drunk for the very first time, my escape route for those explorations in the city, my way home at the end of two years. Now things seemed to be in odd and unexpected places, distances shrunk and then stretched.

The Astra turned into a clearing, and in a moment everything looked the way it should. Here were the billets where I had lived in a previous life, when the months felt like forever. We stopped for a moment and I realized we had parked outside my own block. The giant pointed at the building and told me he lived there during the week. 'Then I go home to Nurnburg,' he said, and the looming soldier with the gun became a suburban commuter with a regional office. I had a moment to notice that the Luftwaffe gargoyles in the leather flying-helmets still gazed out from over the doorway, and then our tour was on the road again.

The mystery of the Gatow Golf Club was soon revealed. It had taken up residence in the building I remembered as the Officers' Mess. It was a transformation which put me in mind of a delicious story I'd heard about Dutch soldiers on NATO exercises going on strike because they were not allowed to wear the hairnets which kept their flowing locks clear of their rifle mechanisms.

Emerging from behind a clump of pine trees, I spotted the monitoring building. It was flanked now by a battery of satellite dishes, but as we cruised past it looked unchanged from the place I remembered. It was frustrating not to be able to get a closer look at my old spy base, but the giant was already heading back to the main gate. As I retrieved my passport, I asked how I might arrange a longer visit. He gave me the phone number of the Luftwaffe Press Office and waved me goodbye. As I drove away, the visit felt unreal, like a dream half remembered the next morning.

Just down the road I saw a sign for the Luftwaffe Museum. The Checkpoint Charlie Museum, the Stasi Museum, and now this – the Cold War was pickled and stored away. I drove through a forest along an empty back road. At the end I passed through a high wire-mesh fence and saw that I was at the far side of the Gatow base. On the old airstrip where the Berlin airlift had once touched down, I could see lines of planes arranged as tidily as Erich Mielke's chairs. I pulled into a huge empty car park. A man came out of a distant Portakabin, pointing and shouting. He insisted that I move the car a few feet. I wondered if he was a redundant Stasi officer.

I bought a ticket from the parking gauleiter, and wandered out on to the airstrip. A slicing wind delivered a brief barrage of hail. The display of retired fighter planes looked forlorn, dented and peeling. They sat on the tarmac, nose to tail like a herd of elephants. As I walked up the line, I scanned the plaques identifying the relics. 'MiG-21', some of them said, and 'SUKHOI'. I realized they were veteran Soviet planes. I had a connection with these things. Some of them could have been the aircraft I was logging from the monitoring centre when they were in the enemy's vanguard. Now they had made their final landing on our doorstep. It felt like some kind of warped metaphor for the futility of the whole Cold War enterprise.

The Gatow control tower which had marshalled the squadrons of relief aircraft during the Berlin airlift was now, inevitably, another museum. A tableau of dummy Soviet air-traffic controllers squatted at dead radios, ghosts from the long-forgotten intercept war which had brought me here. Coming out of a loo, I was pursued by a shrieking attendant. It seemed I had strayed into staff territory, crossing a frontier as fiercely patrolled as the borders of the Cold War. The habits of demarcation were clearly ingrained in these parts.

Heading back for the car, I spotted something at the very edge of the airfield. It seemed oddly familiar, but why? Up against the forest and the fence which had once marked the boundary of the Soviet Zone was a white hut raised on stilts with a ladder leading up to it. Then it flooded back. This had to be the useless Direction Finding Tower, where I had struggled with the rusty wheel and blasted the AFN Jazz Hour into the darkness to blot out the singing Soviet soldiers. Now it was just an old hut, and the fence was just a fence.

23

I WENT TO FIND the Soviet War Memorial near the Brandenburg Gate, where we had chatted to a young Soviet soldier and discovered his bewilderment about the location of Germany. Under a sky the colour of a bruise, with fitful snow and a bitter wind, I found that the memorial had been spruced up. The tanks had a new paint job, green as gherkins, and the heroic Soviet emblem had been regilded.

As I was leaving the memorial, my mobile phone rang. 'This is Mario Benz,' a voice said, 'from the Luftwaffe Press Office.' I still found it surreal that the outfit which had rained bombs on my childhood had a press office, but I was impressed. I had faxed my request for a visit to my old base only the afternoon before, fully expecting a six-week silence before receiving a computerized brush-off. 'When would you like to come?' the voice asked. 'This afternoon?' I almost dropped the phone.

At the gate of General Steinhof Kaserne, a chubby man in a blue uniform was waiting.

'Mario Benz,' he announced, shaking my hand. I

gabbled out my story once again. Mario looked politely puzzled. I realized that the very idea of a British airman living and doing something strange on the base in a time before he was born was just too exotic to grasp. 'Where would you like to go?' he said.

We pulled up in front of my old living block. I sat for a moment on the front steps, replaying a remembered photograph of myself aged twenty. Sitting in that same spot, decked out in my best uniform, I'm smiling. Across the bottom, I've written 'April 1958'. It sticks in my mind because it was one of my very few colour photos from that time. The colours have drained away to sepia now, but I can still see that on that spring day long ago, with demob and the rest of my life ahead of me, I was happy. Now another snow flurry cut short my reverie and I pushed through the familiar door.

The lobby had a startling new occupant. Dominating the immaculate hallway was a huge Coca-Cola machine. It was a visitor from another dimension, suddenly materialized like Dr Who's Tardis. For a moment, I thought I must have remembered the wrong building. But then of course it was just as it should be. We're all Coke people these days.

I went up the stairs, feeling that the years since I'd last tramped up after a long day's sleuthing had shrivelled to nothing. Everything was utterly familiar, the gleaming corridor, the rooms arranged along both sides behind their anonymous doors. I homed in on my old room and knocked on the door. No answer. Further down the corridor, a man built like a phone-box looked out of his doorway. Mario, who seemed to be getting involved with my sentimental journey, went to talk to the man. 'He says OK to look in his room,' Mario reported. The cosy box like the one I'd shared with Ron and Ray was now home for a single Luftwaffe man, and it looked as though it had been invaded by Ikea. A flourishing rubber plant fought for space with a jungle of growing things and an exercise bike. Fitness, the environment, Ikea and Coke – the perfect profile for the virtual military.

Across the road, I looked in on the old cookhouse. It still had its leftover Nazi gargoyle on the wall, a stone relief of a fat cook wearing a chef's hat, a dead ringer for Hermann Goering, I thought. The unvarying cycle of dreary slop had been one of the most resistible features of my time at Gatow. Now the place looked like a Berni Inn, all brasswork and red velvet. It obviously kept the chunky airman across the road well-provisioned.

'Let's go and look at the old monitoring building,' I said. On this winter afternoon, the hulking block looked as glamorous as an old folks' home. Mario sat in his car and left me to wander around. I pushed through the door, expecting some remnant of the old security gates. Instead I was greeted by an even bigger Coke machine. This one seemed calculated to rewrite my entire quest as a Mel Brooks farce. The Coke logo on the front of the machine was circled – impossibly – by a pair of head-phones. It felt like a low-level cosmic joke.

I trudged upstairs to the monitoring floor. There was nothing I recognized. Just a polished wooden floor, white walls, empty rooms. I failed to catch even the faintest echo of what had gone on here in this bright, clean nowhere. The old geography of the place was still inside me. Over there was where the monitoring room had been, where I had hunched in the gloom, listening and scribbling. Back there had been the closed area where our stuff went to be analysed. Now it was all as featureless as a dentist's waiting-room.

I thought: *So Long at the Fair*. In the early fifties I had seen the film, and for some reason it had stuck in my imagination. Jean Simmons, I think, all sweetness in a bustle, is visiting the 1896 Paris Exhibition with her brother. After a day of excitements, they go back to the hotel and say their goodnights. The next morning, the brother has vanished. The hotel people insist the girl arrived alone and they never saw a brother. Even his room isn't there – just an unbroken corridor where the door used to be. Now the monitoring centre felt like that, everything I remembered airbrushed out.

As I recall, the brother's disappearance had something to do with a plague epidemic. Of course the rubbing out of my own spy centre was no mystery. The passage of years, and the ending of the Cold War, had long ago wiped away every trace of what had gone on here.

I had been trying again to give Mario a clearer notion of what I'd been doing at Gatow. He got the idea now, but he didn't seem especially interested. I fancied it must have seemed utterly remote, like being told I had served time in a Roman legion. Then, on the way to the main gate, Mario said: 'I used to be on the crew of a Sukhoi bomber.' So he was a son of Communism, we had been old adversaries. If he'd been a few years older, I could have been listening in on his every move. Somehow, the revelation gave my former life here a jolt of reality.

Driving back into the city, I thought about how little evidence there was in Berlin now of the Cold War drama which had brought me here. Unvisited museums and derelict jet planes, forgotten memorials and scraps of Berlin Wall in plastic bags, the remnants of a vast stand-off which had shaped the world for half a century, looked a lot less substantial than those Coke machines.

24

RAFLING NEWS is a monthly newsletter for former RAF Linguists, hoarding the memories of old boys like me and the 5,000 graduates of the JSSL Hogwarts for junior spooks. It is packed with upbeat reminiscences and accounts of reunions. There are offers of Linguist mugs, and invitations to the unveiling of memorial plaques at Pucklechurch and Crail. There are jokes and poems and anecdotes. There's a crossword with Linguist clues: 'Military fliers akin to swallows'. There's a Padre's Corner, a feature by a Linguist turned man of God which begins: 'Like many, I started with headphones, pencil and pad' and ends: 'There is electronic communication, and most difficult of all, communication with our maker. Let's get switched on then!'

Rafling News showed me a community I had never imagined. Out there were hundreds – thousands perhaps – of men of a certain age who cherished the memory of their time as Linguists. One article recalled 'Halcyon days at Gatow'. I could feel the warmth of the reminiscence, but I couldn't share it. It seemed to have little connection with the reality of what we'd been doing.

For me the JSSL experience stirred different emotions and other questions.

What, in the end, I wondered, had the decades of spying and snooping, the vast accumulation of material about the Cold War enemy really amounted to? Was it all, including the JSSL endeavour, as one sceptical JSSL graduate claimed when I talked to him, little more than an 'expression of paranoid national purpose'? Or was it simply about itself, a chummy freemasonry of National Servicemen whose lives were enriched by learning Russian?

I set out to track down some of the people who had travelled the same road as National Service Linguists in the 1950s. I knew it wasn't going to be simple. Within months of saying goodbye to all that, I had lost contact with almost all my JSSL comrades. The few survivors I still knew were mainly long-standing friends with lives which crossed over mine. Keith had been the best man at my wedding, after dipping in and out of my life from school, through Crail to Cambridge and beyond. We had barely talked about our National Service adventures over the years, but for him too his spell as a Linguist seemed to have been a halcyon period. Always unassailably cheerful, he told me he had fond memories of his time as an Army Linguist, pottering around northern Germany on a motor scooter – 'with pedals', he recalled. Keith put me on to other ageing JSSL pencil-pushers, and the ripples in the pond began to spread.

The people I met up with were a disparate bunch, their stories a sampling of middle-class British lives in the last half of the twentieth century. In a very British way, National Service Linguists had been preselected for a place in some establishment. So it was hardly surprising to find that a generation of grammar-school boys, who had been scooped up by JSSL, had gone on to become teachers and solicitors, textile executives and TV producers. What was more unexpected was to discover the range of JSSL alumni who had gone on to make their marks in the world. I found National Service Linguists had become British Ambassadors, heads of Oxbridge colleges, a bishop, Director of Public Prosecutions, Governor of the Bank of England. There were eminent names from the arts among the JSSL old boys: Alan Bennett, Dennis Potter, Michael Frayn. There was a gaggle of professors, historians and a friar. For all of them, I found, JSSL had somehow touched their lives.

'HE STILL OWES ME eighty quid, and he's been dead five years.' Jim Quick has the instinctive timing of a natural comic, and his torrent of anecdotes about old Linguists was keeping the table bubbling.

I had asked a gang of veteran Linguists to meet me for lunch in London, and half a dozen had braved a London Tube strike to be there. The get-together had been organized by a JSSL Linguist called Graham Boiling, who had graduated from Crail about a year after me. Through a string of emails, I gathered Graham was a moving spirit of a group of ex-Crailites called the East Neuk Luncheon Club, who met up twice a year to swap memories and catch up on scattered lives. 'We enjoy a good meal,' he told me, 'and rehearse tall tales, and remember improbable exploits from long ago.' He said

he'd try to recruit some of the club, and perhaps someone from another group, the Old Gatowians. Added to
the stories in *Rafling News*, it was clear that there was a
network of former JSSL people who, unlike me, had
kept in touch over five decades.

Boiling had sent me the guest list – a snapshot of
what had happened to a group of British youths who
were chosen for their minor roles in the Cold War epic.
There was Gilbert (Crail '58), who went on to work
at GCHQ; John (Crail '57), who had a career in the
Immigration Service and in Customs and Excise; Mike
(Crail '57), who had been with the MOD; Phil (Crail
'58), who worked for Sabena airlines; Jim (Crail '59), who
joined a merchant bank; and Graham (Crail '58), who
spent his working life in the Home Office with spells in
the Foreign Office and the Prison Service.

How far, I wondered, had those lives been re-directed
by the JSSL experience? However that might be, our
shared experience in that spy school still had enough
gravity to pull us from our separate orbits for a few hours
almost half a century later.

They arrived one at a time, like characters introduc-
ing themselves in a little drama. Mike Smallwood was
first, regretting that he had parked his motorbike miles
away when there was a space across the street. 'Crail
'57,' he announced as we shook hands. He told me he'd
had a career in the Ministry of Defence, auditing SIS
accounts, and it seemed something of the bluff military
style had stayed with him. Almost immediately, he
shared a long-standing grievance. 'I came out close to
the top in the final exams at Crail, and I should have

qualified for Cambridge. Then they told me that the Cambridge course had just been wound up, so I missed out.' After the years, I could still feel the force of his disappointment. Like me, Smallwood had been at RAF Gatow, and when he started to tell me about the last time he was in Berlin, that too seemed to be a story tinged with regret. 'It was in 1994,' he said 'on an Old Gatowian reunion.' By chance it turned out to be the weekend when the last Russian soldiers were leaving the city. 'So we tottered off to the East, and spoke to the enemy,' Mike said. 'The Russians were crying, and saying they were going back to nothing, and they'd be paid in cabbages.' He recalled how the East Berliners had written on a bedsheet: 'Thank you Russians for saving us from Fascism!' There was one final exchange with the old enemy. 'The Russian soldiers signed autographs,' Mike said, 'then they marched off with tears in their eyes.'

Graham Boiling arrived, tall and dapper in a green bow tie. In polite deference to my rumpled state, he immediately dismantled the tie. Then the rest turned up, in a flurry of anecdotes about how they had coped with the frustrations of the Tube strike. I looked around the group, thinking how we had all morphed from those fresh-faced youths of my Crail photos, with unguessable lives ahead of us, to this comfortable lunch club of sprightly sixty-somethings with stories to tell.

Most of the group had been getting together like this for years, and I felt like a new boy in school as they swapped news of other old Linguists, of retirements and illnesses and a couple of early deaths. Someone mentioned an old Linguist who had always wanted to be an actor, but had then died just as he was about to go on stage. I had the sense that the prospect I offered of a fresh audience for old anecdotes was as welcome as the meal. I was soon bombarded with memories and stories of Crail and Pucklechurch and Gatow.

'Do you remember the loony instructor at Pucklechurch who went off and murdered his family?' ... 'What about those boozing contests at the Havel Casino near Gatow where you had to drink from a glass boot!' ... 'Then there was Pete the barber at Gatow who turned out to be an East German spy' ... 'Somebody left a turd on the Corporal of the Horse's doorstep' ... 'Do you remember singing rugger songs to the Americans in Berlin?'

Well no, actually I didn't remember any of that. I began to feel I must have been in a parallel universe, a quieter place, shut away from all that naughtiness and drama. Was it really like that, I wondered, or was this just the overheated banter of a reminiscence competition? Maybe it was just that these men had travelled the JSSL road a year after me when times and attitudes were already shifting and relaxing. Maybe it was because by that time men without a degree usually had to 'sign on' as regular servicemen for three years or more to get on to the JSSL course, and so were less desperate to escape.

They talked about a near mutiny when a new Commanding Officer ordered a compulsory cross-country run. Most of the Linguists had abandoned the run after a few yards, and were summoned for a fierce dressing-down. The surly youths greeted the CO's wrath with rebellious murmuring and then with outspoken insubordination. The Commanding Officer wanted to call in the Black Watch to quell the mutiny, but was ordered to back off by his superiors, who wanted qualified Linguists rather than detainees. It was a defiance of service order which seemed inconceivable to me, but it was perhaps revealing of how quickly things were changing in the late 50s. As the stories wound on, I learned new things about how it had been back then for some of those who came after me.

My lunch companions recalled a version of life in Crail which sounded a lot more raffish than the sober language school I remembered. 'I got hold of a couple of washing machines and a tumble dryer,' Jim said, 'and I did brisk business laundering stuff for lads who had been sending their dirty underwear home. Nobody seemed to mind too much that their shirts tended to come out pink. When the Air Force found out, they threatened to sue me for stealing electricity.' John set up his own business dispensing haircuts, slightly less brutal than the Crail barber, for threepence a time. Someone remembered the Siberian Salt Sifters, a skiffle group put together by an enterprising quartet of Linguists who played a regular Friday evening session at the Music Box Café.

When we began to trade memories of Berlin, I had a bit of a shock. There were the now familiar stories of fun and frolics I seemed to have missed – the easy ladies of Spandau known as 'the dwarf', 'the chimp' and 'the horse'; the gays outside the NAAFI club; the drinking binges. But then there were the revelations about the Eierschale – the jazz club where I'd had my minor epiphany. 'It was a favourite honey trap used by the Stasi to seduce naïve young servicemen,' Mike said. 'If you went back to a girl's flat, you would probably be photographed and blackmailed.' So maybe that wild girl with her cardigan back to front was the local Mata Hari, and I'd had a narrow escape. It seemed as improbable as the thought that the friendly beatnik who accused me of looking absurdly English with my tie and blazer was actually a gay agent.

The lunch had reached the strawberry gâteau stage when Graham suddenly asked me if I'd known a man called Peter Hall. 'He must have been at Crail about your time.' Could he be asking about be the same Peter, my soulmate from those trips to the Bottle Dungeon in St Andrews? 'Curly haired chap, plummy voice,' Graham said. So it was the same man. 'Do you have any idea what happened to him?' I asked. 'Yes, I'm surprised you didn't come across him when you were filming in Eastern Europe. Sir Peter was the British Ambassador in Belgrade when the war in the Balkans started.' I wondered if Sir Peter had tried a bit of 'one-upmanship' on Milosevic.

ST ANTONY's College in Oxford, where I had arranged to meet Harold Shukman, was a fitting gathering place for old spooks. An unremarkable collection of Victorian brickwork and Cold War concrete not far from the city centre, St Antony's is a graduate college specializing in international relations, with a particular interest in

Russia and the former Soviet states. Generations of well-informed men with unusual backgrounds have passed through the college, excavating the remarkable library and sharing their knowledge of some of the world's more secretive places.

Sharp at noon, the swing doors swung open and an energetic-looking man in a flowing raincoat came to greet me. Harry Shukman had recently retired as a university lecturer in modern Russian history. He was also one of the earliest graduates of JSSL, and he had co-written a recent history of the National Service Russian Linguists. I thought he might be able to tell me more about the impact of JSSL on the generation who were moulded by it.

Shukman led me into the 'Russian viewing room', an anonymous cell with barred windows. 'I used to watch Russian TV in here when it was worth watching,' he said. We traded the names of mutual Moscow acquaintances, and we swapped recollections of the cockroaches which shared the bedrooms with guests at the Rossiya Hotel just off Red Square.

Shukman's story of how JSSL changed his life was remarkable. I came to understand that it also spoke for hundreds of other JSSL graduates whose lives were transformed by learning Russian in the Forces. At school, he had been at the bottom of his class, thirty-second out of thirty-three. 'I had no serious secondary education,' he recalled, 'and I trained to be a radio engineer in a factory.' At his RAF selection interview, Shukman was told he could train to become a Russian interpreter because he had Russian parents. 'So the assumption was that I could speak Russian, which was a totally false assumption. My parents didn't speak Russian at home, none of the family spoke Russian.'

Shukman told me how he went off to give the good news of his Linguist's training to an uncle. 'He was a communist in the early 1950s, a very hard-line Stalinist. And he was very upset. He said: 'They're going to train you to spy on your own people.' For the young Shukman, it was a shock. 'That was the first thought I ever had that this was some kind of spying.'

But for all the suspicions, as an RAF Linguist on an early course in the winter of 1952, Shukman found his vocation. 'I just loved doing it. I think I was like a sponge that had never been filled.' Within months, the schoolboy failure who had not even been entered for an eleven plus grammar school exam had won a place to continue his National Service Russian at Cambridge University. Shukman recalled the Cambridge of the early 50s with the kind of rapture Evelyn Waugh had given his young men in the Oxford of *Brideshead Revisited*. There was the punting, of course, but much more besides. 'It was a lovely experience. There was a café in the middle of Cambridge called the Dorothy. It had a tea dance in the afternoons with music, and with any luck you might pick up a Scandinavian au pair to dance with while you had your tea and crumpets.' Shukman acted in Russian-language productions of Chekhov; he relished lectures on Russian history and philosophy. 'It was very difficult to remember you were in the RAF.'

Shukman did recall some token military business towards the end of his National Service. 'We were told we would be trained to interrogate Soviet prisoners of war. And we had a session on interrogation – that consisted of being made to say "Name, rank and serial number", and that was it. You couldn't go beyond that because the Geneva Convention said you couldn't subject them to the third degree or anything.' The prospect of those exercises ever becoming real was clearly remote. 'I certainly had no thought that one day I might be sitting in a darkened room with a spotlight on a prisoner.'

We went upstairs for lunch in the college common room. Shukman introduced me to a dapper colonel in a tweed sports jacket and perfectly polished shoes. We exchanged experiences in the guarded language of old spooks who can't be entirely sure about the other chap, and the man in the shiny shoes got my attention with a recital of his many 'intelligence assignments'. 'The Russian Linguist business is still going on,' he wanted me to know. 'These days, a lot of it has to do with arms control.' I got the impression there might be other things the Linguists were doing these days, too.

Over coffee, Shukman was frank about the value of the Cambridge interpreters' experience. 'Certainly it didn't justify itself if you're looking purely at the defence aspect.' But he had a striking suggestion about the long-term potential of the training. 'We were prepared like nuclear weapons,' he said. 'In readiness but never actually used.' He was sure as well about an unintended bonus of the JSSL experiment. 'Five thousand people were trained in the Russian language, and many of them retained an interest in things Russian, and in what was going on in

Russia. It did help to create a more informed element in Soviet–British relations.'

But whatever the effect on Cold War relations, the impact of JSSL on the twenty-one-year-old Harry Shukman was dramatic. 'The Russian Course totally transformed my life,' he said. 'I wasn't really on track to do anything. JSSL was the rocket motor that actually put me into orbit.' Armed with his Russian language skills, after demob Shukman got a place at university and left his radio apprenticeship behind. The boy who was forgotten at the bottom of the class went on to become an Oxford professor. It sounds like a heart-warming fable from some 1950s rags-to-riches film, but for him it came true.

I MET OTHER JSSL people who had remarkably similar stories. Ted Braun told me: 'It absolutely transformed my life, because I was going nowhere when I left school.' His RAF Russian earned him a place at Cambridge, and he went on to become Professor of Drama at Bristol University.

Gerry Smith was sure he had no interest in Russia or Russian, but he went to JSSL because 'maybe I'd get some time to practise the saxophone'. Like Shukman, Smith got hooked. The Manchester boy who dreamed of playing jazz and becoming an engineer is now Professor of Russian at Oxford. 'It became my whole life,' he said. As we finished our talk, from a back room he unearthed an old case. Nestling inside, like a precious Russian ikon, was his alto sax.

I was beginning to feel a bit like a member of a born-again sect. I had never imagined that so many of my fellow Linguists would say that they had been rescued by the JSSL experience.

I HAD BRIEFLY met the playwright and novelist Michael Frayn years ago, but I hadn't been aware then that he had any connection with JSSL. He had been a bit ahead of my time, a graduate of an earlier course at Bodmin in Cornwall, and became one of the high flyers who went on to polish up his Russian at Cambridge. I had just finished reading *Spies*, Frayn's latest novel, about espionage during World War II seen through the eyes of a child, which had a haunting resonance for me.

He had a clear memory of the moment when he was told he had been selected. The gangling Frayn had found himself standing in front of the selection officer in filthy denims, alongside a tiny fellow conscript – 'Like a comic duo,' he recalled. 'You may think this is a skive,' the officer said, 'but in fact it's a very serious choice. If you're trained as a Russian interpreter, you may find yourself at any moment dropped by parachute behind enemy lines.' Frayn leaned back, relishing the memory. Then he said: 'This didn't happen.'

For Linguists like me who had said goodbye to our cleverer friends at the end of basic language training, the life of those who had gone on to continue their Russian at university had always been the stuff of envy and speculation. This was my chance to revisit some envious speculation. 'We had this vision,' I told him, 'of you gliding around in punts with floozies and chilled white wine.' Losing my nerve a bit, I conceded: 'I guess that wasn't wholly accurate.' I had asked, and Frayn did not spare me the shocking truth. 'I did actually learn to punt when I was on the Russian course at Cambridge. After lunch on Friday, you were paid in cash and then you were free. You had five pounds in your pocket, so you were like some millionaire undergraduate released into Cambridge. And that's when we did the punting.'

Before my long-dormant class envy could get the better of me, Frayn had some less idyllic news about the Cambridge course. 'We worked like mad. There was a test every Friday morning, and if you failed the test you got returned to unit.' In other words, you would be kicked out of Eden and required to swap your punting-pole for a scrubbing-brush. Much worse, you could find yourself fighting in the swamps of Malaya. 'I recall working fourteen hours a day,' Frayn said. It still sounded like more fun than scribbling away in the monitoring room, but I wondered if the élite Linguists had been given any more idea than the rest of us about how they fitted into the bigger picture of Cold War intelligence gathering. 'I don't think any of us had the faintest clue, or indeed very much interest in where all this would end up,' Frayn said. There was some talk about interrogating prisoners, it seems, but no further mention of alarming parachute drops. This was just as well, he felt. 'We were not really good Linguists, and if we'd been dropped behind Russian lines at any point, the very first time we opened our mouths would have been the end of our careers.' Frayn threw his head back and laughed at the awful fantasy.

A THIN DRIZZLE was beginning as I stood waiting in the street. This backwater in North London, a nowhere of tarted-up warehouses and parked cars, was made even more resolutely drab by the gunmetal grey skies of a sultry July afternoon. I saw a man cycling towards me, and even under the improbable crash helmet there was no mistaking the national treasure. Alan Bennett wobbled to a halt, and hauled a jacket out of the basket strapped to his handlebars. With his shock of hair and perpetual schoolboy's face, he said hello in a Yorkshire accent which could only have been bred within biking distance of Market Balcony. I helped him drag the bike into a lift, and we squashed in alongside it, finding things to say. I thought: 'This is a scene from an Alan Bennett story.'

Bennett was another of the 5,000 graduates of JSSL. I had written to him a few years back to suggest that he might write a play about the Linguist phenomenon. In my letter I had hinted at our shared boyhoods – both growing up in the West Riding after the war, both living over the parents' shop, both learning Russian during National Service, both going on as grammar school boys to Oxbridge. In fact it wasn't as shameless a pitch as it might have appeared. I had often felt a strong affinity with Bennett, and his ear for the conversation which had been the soundtrack of my youth sometimes made me feel that he had been bugging my daily doings. Coming upon his account of a Yorkshire matron 'rooting' in her handbag, I was back in our kitchen, fretting as my mother excavated interminably for her ever-elusive glasses.

I had received a treasured postcard in reply to my letter. It sits on my shelf to this day. On one side is a photo of a gritty hillside in the Yorkshire Dales, the summit obscured in dirty clouds. On the reverse, Bennett has written in neat black fountain pen: 'I'm sure my Aunt Eveline would have known your Dad's music shop. She was a pianist for the silent films, and we still have all her music.' He didn't think the Linguist experience was his dramatic cup of tea. 'I live opposite Michael Frayn who was also on it – it's much more his kind of thing. But I'll bear it in mind (staring out of the window at the moment).'

Bennett had agreed to chat about his memories of JSSL in the office which is my base for TV work. As he propped up his bike in the gap between some unoccupied desks and pulled off his cycle clips, young women peeped out of doors for a glimpse of the unlikely celebrity. No one was quite bold enough to risk their cool and ask for an autograph.

Bennett is a few years older than me and I wondered how it had been for him, back then in 1952, finding his way on to the Russian course. 'It was known that the Russian course was a skive, and a cushy number. It didn't turn out to be quite as idyllic as legend made out, but it was certainly far better than being sent to the front in Korea.'

Unlike me, though, Bennett made it to the Cambridge Linguists' course. Like Michael Frayn, whom he met on the Cambridge course, he still remembers it as being one of the happiest times in his life.

'I enjoyed it far more, really, than I did when I went

to university proper. It was the first time I'd been away from home, the first time I'd been with people from other backgrounds. I was certainly a bit daunted by how clever some of them were.' Bennett added with a chuckle: 'You realized what a sheltered life you'd led until that time.' Along with imbibing the glories of Russian literature, he recalls how he and his 'exuberantly clever' fellow Linguists had to crawl through thickets of military jargon. 'I always remember "rolling barrage". I had a notion it was something that rolled. I didn't realize it was guns. I thought it was some sort of juggernaut.'

I had come across a marvellous photograph of teenagers Bennett and Frayn with their bikes on a Cambridge lane, taking time off from the tussle with Soviet military jargon. The sun is shining and they look impossibly young. It's a picture which seems utterly removed from any possibility of spying or the prospect of parachuting into Russia. I told Bennett about his old cycling companion's notions of being dropped behind enemy lines. 'I think that's fantasy,' he said, exploding with laughter. 'If anybody had suggested parachuting to me, I think I would have been rather nervous.' I had to admit that the image of Britain's treasure diving from a plane and drifting down into hostile territory wasn't easy to summon up.

I asked Alan Bennett what he made of the whole enterprise. Did he think we Linguists had actually made any difference? He had a surprising answer. 'I've always thought,' he said, 'not just about the Russian course, but also about the Cambridge spies, the more spying there is the better. The more one side knows about the other, the safer the world will be'. Then he added: 'I still don't feel that treason is the highest crime.'

Of course it should not have surprised me. Bennett's sad and funny play *An Englishman Abroad*, about the superspy Guy Burgess, stranded in Moscow with only the *Times* crossword, a Jane Austen novel and a Jack Buchanan record for company, had presented an unforgettably human version of the old traitor. Bennett had written in an introduction to the play: 'I find it hard to drum up any patriotic indignation over Burgess or Blunt or even Philby. The trouble with treachery nowadays is that if one does want to betray one's country, there's no one satisfactory to betray it to.'

KEN TRODD and I had worked at Granada TV at the same time in the 1970s. He was a successful and famously acerbic producer of gritty, politically relevant dramas, who had gone on to produce some of of the most celebrated and controversial plays in television history, including a string of remarkable plays by Dennis Potter.

By chance, as I pursued my quest for old Linguists, Trodd called me. He wanted my opinion on a writer I had worked with, and before we said goodbye for a few more years he asked what I was up to. 'I'm trying to track down people who learned Russian during National Service like me,' I said, expecting no more than polite interest. 'My God – you did that too,' he said, and then told me he had his own JSSL story. It emerged that he'd done the Russian course ahead of me, and along the way he'd met up with a rebellious young Army private called

Dennis Potter. We agreed to get together and swap stories.

Trodd had hardly changed, I thought. Under the greenish strip lights in a TV office where he was starting another production, he still had something of the austerity of a monk, his face gaunt and carved into sharp angles. And he still had the seditious eloquence of a lifelong class warrior. He recalled with obvious pleasure how he and Potter had contrived to beat the JSSL system fifty years ago. 'We weren't allowed to go to the waters of Cambridge,' he said with a bleak little smile, 'but we did achieve something which no one else in our batch achieved. I think we did something in the clerk's office, some little piece of persuasion and/or chicanery to get us to London.'

So instead of ending up crouched over a radio on a rainswept German hilltop, Trodd and Potter were posted to the War Office in Whitehall. Their daily job was to sift through the contents of Soviet waste bins – and worse – as footsoldiers in 'Operation Tamarisk'. There was something utterly appropriate about the vision of a pair of Britain's angriest young men trawling for secrets in the sewers of the Cold War. Trodd's recollections of decoding the mysteries wrapped up in used Soviet loo paper remained vivid. 'Day after day, there was this stuff. Exactly how it routed itself to Whitehall virtually overnight, I never knew.'

What Trodd and Potter seemed to have taken most memorably from their Linguist experience, apart from those close encounters with the bowels of Socialism, was a sharpened class awareness. He still recalled with obvious relish the satisfaction of observing the toffs who were their Whitehall supervisors. 'In that War Office, surrounded by members of our upper class, we felt we were spies in a double sense. We were working as spies on behalf of the West. We were also spies in the environment of the English upper class, who would never have encountered us, or wanted to, had we not been in that situation.' Then he added some thoughts that might have been tailored to illuminate my own sense of my life as a spy: 'You're in an alien world, you're in a secret world. You're working for their secrets, but you're also somehow preserving your own.'

I asked Trodd what he thought it all added up to, this strange business of force-feeding the language of the Cold War enemy, eavesdropping on his every twitch, decoding his toilet paper. Did it perhaps keep us from some apocalyptic misunderstanding which could have provoked nuclear war? 'It did maintain a kind of weird and silly status quo, I suppose,' he said. 'But if there hadn't been any Russian courses, would that have made any difference?'

THROUGH FRIENDS in Moscow, I tried to track down a counterpart, someone who had been listening in on us while we tuned in to them. I got nowhere. The well-connected friends reported that Mr Putin's Russia was not keen on opening up espionage files, even archives from fifty years ago. A former Linguist told me that an officer in the Yugoslav army had informed him that 'the Russians knew more about what you were doing than you ever realized'. But with a former KGB man in the

Kremlin, the twenty-first-century version of the KGB was now back in charge. The brief flirtations with free information of the early 1990s were a thing of the past. For a while Matreshka, those nests of dolls within dolls on sale at every Moscow street corner, offered tourists to Russia a witty shorthand summary of recent Soviet history. Yeltsin nestled inside Gorby inside Brezhnev inside Krushchev, with a tiny Stalin doll at the heart of it all. Now the Matreshka of Soviet spying during the Cold War had been glued shut, holding its layers and secrets to itself.

There were times during my efforts to excavate the meaning of my own intelligence story when its inner workings seemed just as inaccessible. Then I found an insider. Ted Braun was a Gatow veteran, and he'd had access to those back rooms in the monitoring centre where my raw material was digested and reprocessed. I wanted to talk to him about how the stuff was used and whether he thought it had any value. Braun is an affable man with a cropped grizzled beard. I had seen a photograph of him when he'd been a young RAF officer at Gatow and looked a bit like the British 50s heart-throb Michael Wilding. Unlike most other JSSL people, he was not a National Service man. He had signed on for five years in the hope of redeeming a disappointing school career and getting on to the Russian course.

Braun's JSSL career had followed a more rarefied trajectory than mine. He told me he had even had a batman when he spent a few months at Crail, a former fisherman from the village. But he had ended up at Gatow at around the same time I was there. I think he may even have been in that back room processing my very raw material. I was intrigued to know what it meant to him and the other analysts. 'What we were looking for were abnormal activities,' he said. 'Changes in air chatter which indicated the introduction of new kind of aircraft, and most importantly, any kind of incident.' Braun told me how the British and Americans would try to provoke those incidents by sending planes, known as 'Ferrets', along the air corridors and straying intentionally into East German air space. 'It was very exciting when one of these happened,' he said, lighting up at the memory, 'because you people were logging these messages, and the chatter was quite out of the ordinary.' Of course I had been entirely unaware of these dangerous games being played out over our heads in order to provide us scribblers with juicy fodder. Hearing about it now gave me a frisson about the risks of those Cold War cat-and-mouse adventures – when the cat and the mouse both possessed nuclear claws. And I certainly wasn't sure that the material harvested by my imperfect logging was worth the risk of provoking World War III.

HAPPILY, Ted Braun had some less alarming stories about what we'd been doing at Gatow. 'Every month or so there was a change in the callsigns of the enemy pilots and their ground stations,' he said. It seemed a key part of our job was to try to record those changes so that the people ranged above us, presumably from the back room down the corridor at the monitoring building to Downing Street and the White House, could get a snapshot of what the Reds might be up to. Fortunately,

Braun recalls, the Commie pilots were as fallible as we were. 'Pilots frequently made mistakes,' he said, 'so you would hear something like: "Strawberry 105 calling!" And then he'd say, "Fuck it! I mean Gooseberry 565". So you immediately know that "Strawberry" becomes "Gooseberry", and the 100s become the 560s.'

I can't recall being aware of this Cold War parlour game at the time. But Ted Braun insisted that, however unknowingly, the Linguist toilers in the monitoring centre had done something. 'I was often in awe of the skills of you young guys, sitting there with your headphones on – what you managed to get down.'

After more than four decades, I suppose it was some kind of delayed pat on the back.

THE VOICE on the phone was instantly familiar. Sir Peter Hall KBE, CMG sounded eerily like Aircraftman Second Class Hall P., relishing some new absurdity of military routine in our billet at Crail forty-seven years earlier. Following the revelation during my rendezvous with the gang of old Linguists that Peter had gone on to become our man in Belgrade, I had tracked him down. He told me he was retired now, but the JSSL experience had stayed with him as his diplomatic career took him from Delhi to Caracas and Argentina.

I asked Peter if he had ever needed to use his Russian. 'Inevitably, the Foreign Office sent me off on my first diplomatic posting in the early 60s to Warsaw,' he said, 'the one place in the world where speaking Russian was unwelcome.' He also had a typically bizarre story. 'I was on a cruise liner with a largely Ukrainian crew when my wife and I found we needed extra coathangers. From the distant recesses of my Russian vocabulary lists, I dredged up "wyeshalka".' Peter said the steward looked startled. So was I. Coathangers had not featured in our dour military word lists in Berlin. But I thought it was an agreeable footnote to the JSSL enterprise that it had helped an old Linguist to hang up his jacket.

(**25**)

IT ALL SEEMS so long ago now, that world of Cold War stand-off which collided with my life. The rhetoric of confrontation, of 'Evil Empire' and 'Imperialist Aggressor', already feels as quaint as a Mao badge or a Beatles wig. But with the collapse of Communism, some of the workings of the spy machines have been revealed.

I made a final journey to meet a man who knows as much as anyone about those workings. Nottingham University is an agreeable place, set amid a pleasant campus of rolling lawns. On a fine day in early summer, it seemed utterly removed from the brooding suspicions and nuclear terrors of the Cold War. Tracking down Richard Aldrich, I followed his directions and headed past a bronze statue of D. H. Lawrence to the School of Politics. Aldrich is a Professor of Politics at Nottingham University, and a renowned specialist in Cold War intelligence. I found him in his office, an affable balding man who greeted me with apologies for wearing shorts.

He immediately challenged my scepticism about the role of spies and spying in the Cold War. 'The intelligence services were the cutting edge of the Cold War,' he insisted. 'In any sense that the Cold War was fought, the Secret Services were absolutely at the front of that.' As the sound of a lawnmower drifted through the open window, Aldrich reminded me of the terrible stakes of that war. 'We were living in a very dangerous environment among weapons which could have wiped out humanity several times over. Each side was watching the other day and night, and the intelligence services continually provided reassurance to each side that no attack was impending.'

Aldrich was also certain that I had been in the right place at the right time. 'Berlin is absolutely critical to espionage during the the 1950s,' he said, 'because what Berlin offers the West is an out-station inside Eastern Europe.' The juicy eavesdropping potential of the city's location made Aldrich almost lyrical about my old posting. 'It allows the British and the Americans an island of electronic espionage, a large ear right inside the heartland of Soviet armed forces, and there's nothing the Soviets can do about this.'

I told Aldrich about Kenith Trodd's squalid first-hand encounters with Operation Tamarisk, decoding that improvised Soviet toilet paper at his desk in Whitehall. He was clearly delighted to hear of a personal experience of the operation. 'It's fascinating these pieces come together,' he said. 'I actually found the loo paper story in the archive of an American War College, but it's amazing to hear that kind of confirmation.' For all its grimy processes, Aldrich was sure about the importance of the Brixmis 'shit-digging'. 'Operation Tamarisk was perhaps the longest and one of the most productive intelligence operations run by the British during the Cold War,' he said. 'Those used pieces of Russian toilet paper were absolute gold dust in terms of the information they contained.' I made a note to let Trodd know that his ghastly labours had not been in vain.

Most of all, of course, I wanted to talk to Aldrich about my own experience as a mini-spy. His estimate of our plane-spotting could have made me blush. 'That monitoring of Soviet pilots was absolutely critical for East–West reassurance. And if you look at high-level British intelligence analyses of the time, they are remarkably dependent on the monitoring of voice traffic for any indication that war might be imminent.' Aldrich had a vivid image to describe the purpose of our piled-up hours in the monitoring centre. 'Any large animal makes a noise when it moves,' he said, 'and the Soviet armed forces are a very large animal. Essentially what you were doing was listening out for any unusual rustling in the jungle as this animal begins to assume an attack posture.'

That picture of me and my fellow scribblers as intrepid big-game hunters was hard to align with my memories of doing the job, shuffling the carbon paper and recording those routine listings of callsigns and exercises. But Aldrich insisted that was the whole point. 'It's absolutely crucial that the day-to-day monitoring goes on, because that's how you establish your norm. That's what the Soviet armed forces look like when they're not doing anything. And as soon as they do start to do something, there are aberrations, and you pick those aberrations up.' I was still puzzled about how those mundane exchanges about fuel warning lights and undercarriage deployment could deliver so much juice to our unseen spookmasters. 'It's not what's contained in the messages,' Aldrich said, 'it's the number of messages, it's the volume of information which is going to give the Soviets away.'

It was for me a revelation of what I had been doing as a footsoldier in the Cold War. Why, I wondered, had no one in the higher circles of spookery ever let us in on this stuff? Aldrich had suggested that 'a secret service has secrecy as its principal armament'. Still, I thought, any leaking of the tiny secrets at my disposal would hardly have shaken the free world. Did the cult of secrecy really have to include concealing the purpose of what we were doing from the people who were doing it?

They were of course questions from another age, and another life. But Aldrich also had some notions which came closer to home when we talked about the sharing of intelligence with our special relations. 'Intelligence is a form of power,' he suggested. 'And the most important part of Britain's intelligence power is its relationship with the United States. A lot of intelligence operations by the British were carried out in order to justify that relationship.' But Aldrich saw an even broader importance for Britain's spy trade. 'Intelligence power allows Britain to punch above its weight throughout the twentieth century,' he said. 'In fact,' he went on, 'one of the reasons that Britain is a substantial medium power today and not a power like Belgium or Spain has to do with its proficiency in the world of secret intelligence.'

As we came to the end of our talk, Aldrich had one more surprise. It seemed that he shared Alan Bennett's favourable valuation of the spying trade. 'I think the intelligence agencies, which are often seen as the masters of secrecy and deception were more believable than anybody else during the Cold War,' he said. 'Information that was stolen from the enemy was much more believable than the stuff they were giving you themselves.'

GOING INTO Halifax, I got lost. The steep hill down into the town seemed to have been smoothed out. Nothing seemed to be where it should be, everything appeared to have shrunk. The soot-grimed relics of my youth had somehow been traded in for these confident honey-coloured treasures of the Victorian era.

I parked in a multi-storey which had invaded the squalid Dickensian terraces where I used to deliver Christmas mail as a schoolboy temp, and walked into Market Street. I knew that the town had become home for new communities, but I was unprepared for the transformation of the people on the street. Instead of my remembered cast of dour Yorkshire folk, as uniformly pasty as me, I was now rubbing shoulders with Yorkshire tykes in saris and turbans and headscarves. It looked a lot more interesting than the Market Street I used to look out on from our living-room.

My parents' music shop is now a fast-photo outlet. The window, which had been arrayed with saxophones and trumpets and guitars, is plastered with Day-Glo hoardings pushing offers of '20-minute processing'. My mother's record shop has been reborn as a greetings card boutique. Maybe she'd have preferred that – the quiet routines of selling happy birthday cards and sparkly wrapping paper instead of the daily challenge of dealing with pushy teenagers and maddening record buyers who could never remember the title or who it was by.

Along the street, where the stairway to Market Balcony had been, I ran into a locked door. It was protected by a formidable keypad. What could they be doing on Market Balcony these days which needed security? Was there an illicit vegetable scam operating out of the market? I went in search of a way through the door.

The stairs up to the market offices were as steep as a Himalayan track. The chaotic Dickensian room where I'd been directed to enquire about access to my boyhood was a packed time capsule, delivering a rush of memories as I waited. Chipped paintwork in that boiled-cabbage green which haunted my youth, files spilling off wonky shelves, the Victorian wrought-iron pillars glimpsed through grimy widows – the office was like a memorial to the years when this was my world. The only hint that this was another time was a hectoring plaque reminding the workforce that 'Perfect Planning Prevents Pathetic Performance'. A couple of electricians were fretting in a corner, trying to sort out a tangle of wires. 'They have three sockets in this place with forty-seven adaptors,' one sparks lamented into his mobile phone. The friendly secretary asked me: 'Do you want cold water or ordinary?' It was all utterly familiar.

As I waited, I had a look at the most recent catch in my trawl for the story of my National Service. I had sent off to the RAF for my official records, and as I was leaving home to head back to Halifax that morning, a large brown envelope stamped 'On Her Majesty's Service' had flopped through my letter-box. With a few minutes to fill now, I opened the envelope. A letter from a Mrs Wright at the RAF Personnel Management Agency in Gloucester advised me that almost all my documents had long ago been destroyed. 'However,' she wrote, 'your RAF Form 543 "Record of Service" is still held, and a copy of this is attached.'

The colour photocopy, faithfully yellowed and fading at the edges, connected powerfully for me with the shabby market office where I was waiting for admission to the territory of my youth. The details of my National Service, laboriously handwritten with fountain pens by a series of clerks, spelled out my story: 'Report 30 Course of Russian trng. held at JSSL Crail, 12/11/56.' West Malling, Pucklechurch, even my misdirected few hours at Ruislip were itemized. But my time in Berlin was smuggled behind the cryptic code '1/10/57: 3 Det.' A spatter of evasive letters and numbers tracked my way to the magical shorthand 'Disch. 19/7/58.'

As I reviewed my National Service records more closely, I got a shock. In a top corner, a red stamp declared 'Discharged from Class G reserve on 27/2/64.' The message sunk in: 1964 – for six years after I ended my life as a spy, I could still have been sucked back.

For decades after the end of my National Service, I had repeating dreams that I was still held in some RAF stockade. I was often tangled in the feeling that I had escaped my military life, but it had somehow reclaimed me and I couldn't get free. Then I would come awake, washed with relief that it wasn't true.

Now my Service Record was telling me that for half a dozen years, those dreams had been documentaries, messages from a reality I didn't know about. Discovering that possibility for the first time in a place haunted by so many memories gave me a chill. If National Service could reclaim me, perhaps the local demons of Market Balcony could get to me too.

After a while, a chubby man in a T-shirt came to collect me. 'I used to live on Market Balcony until a couple of years ago,' he said, as he led me down the steep stairs and into the street. Alongside the archway into the covered market, he opened a metal door I couldn't remember ever having seen before. We tramped up a dingy stairway and he chattered about how there used to be a mirror shop here. The Mirror Shop! It had been a perpetual hazard of my childhood landscape, the place which disgorged newly resilvered sheets of glass, dripping with acid, to stew on a wooden platform at the end of Market Balcony. I used to dread losing my tennis ball under the platform, fearful that an acid attack might melt me like a victim in one of those films about bodysnatchers from outer space.

And then I was back where I began, outside our door, 22 Market Balcony. The door was painted a cheery red now, and the kitchen windows had been smartened up with artificial leading. A pot with a dead plant was propped on the windowsill above a decorative wheel-barrow with a broken wheel, containing another dead plant. There was no one around, so I peered through the window. The kitchen was as gloomy as ever and I couldn't see much. It looked very yellow in there.

It was half a century ago, but I felt I had hardly been away. Everything was just as I remembered – the looming terrace of flats, the strip of tarmac, the wall of the covered market. Standing alone now on Market Balcony, it came to me how this place defined a special territory in my interior landscape. The high walls and dead ends hemmed me in. It had about it, I realized now, the confines of a cell, and it made me desperate to escape. Suddenly, it contained my long-hoarded feelings about National Service, and life behind the Berlin Wall, and my growing up here.

I was about to look for my crack in the wall when I saw that a small blonde woman was coming towards me. She looked weary, I thought. Burdened with her shopping bags, I wasn't sure she had seen me. Then she said, 'Hello,' seemingly unsurprised to find me there. She found her key and opened the door – my door. In a rush, I told her I used to live here, and asked if I could just take a brief look round. She invited me in, a spy coming back to snoop on his own territory.

I was back in the kitchen where I toiled over my homework, where my father filled those yawning Sundays ordering records, where my mother cooked up the beans and chips, where I watched the men set up our first TV. Everything was surfaced in lime-yellow Formica now, muffling my memory. Still, something lingered, just out of reach.

'Would you like to see the living-room?' the woman asked. Feeling numb, I followed her. A doorway which used to lead down to the shop was sealed up, papered over. The door to my parents' bedroom had gone as well. This was where my father had relished *Grand Hotel* on the radio, where I had toiled over my homework and made model ships. Aunts and uncles had come from miles away to watch the Queen's coronation here, balancing plates of sandwiches on their knees. I had once had a snooker table in here. 'We're planning to move out,' the woman was saying. 'It's so noisy over the street with all the buses.' I remember the buses; but I couldn't imagine just deciding to move out. How could you do that? 'I collect dolls,' the woman said, and they were everywhere, sitting on ledges round the room, gazing down on the intruder. I wanted to be gone.

Outside again on Market Balcony, I had one more thing to do. Where was the crack in the wall? I found the place, but it wasn't there any more. A sheet of glass had been installed, and my spy hole was tidied away now. I peered through the glass, and I was a juvenile spy again, looking down on the world – like it used to be, seeing and not being seen. Improbably, most of the names on the stalls seemed to be the same: Arthur Worsman's vegetables, Whittaker's meats, Coletta's ice cream. The handsome Victorian clock which had marked my boyhood hours was still there. It was getting late now, and the stalls were shutting up for the night.